HECTOR MASSEY lives and farms in Bolton, near Toronto, and teaches political science at York University. A concerned citizen, he decided to align himself with the people of Pickering against the destruction of their property. He was educated at Toronto and McMaster universities. He edited *The Canadian Military: a Profile.*

CHARLES GODFREY is a physician, a professor at the University of Toronto, and a farmer — living in the Uxbridge area. He is the chairman of People or Planes and the most outspoken opponent of the new Toronto airport. He is the author of *The Cholera Epidemics in Upper Canada* and is writing a history of medicine in Ontario.

This is a book about Pickering, an historic southern Ontario community now living under the sentence of death. It is a protest against what many Canadians believe to be an unfair decision, and an appeal by the condemned to Canadian public opinion. In the course of human events there are times when a beleaguered people must stand up and be heard or be forever silent. Such is the feeling of large numbers of people battling against the site chosen for Toronto's second international airport.

PEOPLE
OR
PLANES

HECTOR MASSEY

and

CHARLES GODFREY

The Copp Clark Publishing Company

Toronto   Montreal   Vancouver

HE
797
5

ISBN 0-7730-4009-9

22
55

Printed and bound in Canada

AUTHORS' NOTE

The authors wish to record their thanks to many members of People or Planes including Don Wonnacott, William Leach, Ken Fallis, William Lishman, Clark Muirhead, John Budden, John Coates, Milton Mowbray, Roger Conant, Judge T. Moore, Anne Wanstall, Isobel Thompson, Helen Dennis, Helen Auld, Derek Maw, Ed Falkenberg, Al Graham, Brian Buckles, Dick Elmer, Margaret Godfrey, Dawn Lea, Ian Hamer, and Peter McCowan.

Special thanks are due to Phil Bienhacker of Kates Peat Marwick & Co., Susan Walker of CTV, and John Zaritsky and Hugh Winsor of the *Globe and Mail.* The following government officials went beyond the call of duty in giving of their time and providing helpful insights: in Ontario, Don Stevenson, Assistant Deputy Minister, Department of Economics, and Ken Foley, Research Director, Department of Communication and Transportation; federally, Allan Baker, Special Assistant to Donald Jamieson, Minister of Transport. A number of other government officials at Queen's Park and Ottawa co-operated but wish to remain anonymous.

The authors wish to single out Lorne Almack of People or Planes, Paul Irwin of Copp Clark, and Charles Kahn, freelance editor, for their sterling assistance, without which this little book would not have seen the light of day.

Grateful acknowledgement is made to all concerned for permission to use excerpts from current periodicals and newspapers.

Hector Massey
Charles Godfrey
October 1, 1972

CONTENTS

1. The Community

Hugh John Miller awoke at his usual time on March 2, 1972. Cattle and sheep to feed, chores to do, and up before daybreak. He still used horses on the land in the growing season and stalls were to be cleaned out today.

The snow was heavy and he might have to plow out the lane as he had for fifty years before.

That day he heard about the airport. The government was going to expropriate his farm and build an airport.

John Miller, Hugh John's grandfather, had come to Pickering from Annan, Dumfriesshire, Scotland, in 1835. He and his wife had spent forty-nine days on the sea to New York. They then took a steamboat to Albany, travelled through the Erie Canal to Rochester, and continued across Lake Ontario by boat to Toronto where friends met them and took them in wagons through the woods to Brougham. There he settled on Atha Farm, Lot 25, Concession 7, and hewed out a comfortable home and raised cattle.

In those early days he earned a name as a breeder of livestock. His brother John became Pickering's most famous breeder of shorthorns and sheep. The family owned 350 acres on Concession 7. His Clydesdales were famous throughout the province.

The town of Brougham grew with the Millers. A livery stable and hotel were built in 1850, the townhall in 1854, a new church in 1869, and the Temperance Hall in 1880.

Hugh John and his brother, Robert, who owned a welding and blacksmith shop in Brougham, drove their first tractors, by steam propulsion, on the family farm "Thistle Ha' " in the twenties.

And now the government was going to take his farm and the graves of the generations of Millers over the past 140 years and the homes they had left and the trees they had planted. Hugh John Miller accepted an invitation to act as provisional chairman of a committee to oppose the airport. The first meeting was called for the night of March 2nd. It was held just across the road from the Millers' farm at Melody Farm where Matthew Lount, a rebel who was executed by the government in 1837, had lived.

The Township of Pickering is northeast of Toronto and is within a fifty-mile radius of the city. In preglacial times, this was part of a continental plain, but after the glacial age, the area was permanently configured. To the north looms the Oak Ridges Moraine, known as the Uxbridge Sandhills, a watershed which gives rise to the Rouge River, Duffins Creek, and numerous small streams. Further south are a number of drumlins — oval hills thrown up by the receding glaciers from the surrounding plain. From the high land in the north with its ski hills there is a drop to the rolling tentile plains of the south. Claremont, with a series of valleys, rushing streams, and tree-covered hills is the transition point. Further south the land becomes flatter, and the shallow clay plain is one of the most picturesque farming areas in southern Ontario. To the very south is the lakeshore, a sandy area with boulder trees, and the mouths of several rivers.

The land is Peel clay loam, Woburn clay loam, and Milliken loam — all Class 1 as reported by the Canada Land Inventory. Class 1 represents the highest productivity while class 7 is lowest. Only 11 1/2 per cent of all Ontario lands falls within class 1 and the Pickering area is in this category. Ninety per cent of the land is arable. The remaining 10 per cent is woodlots, ravines, and streams. The area is in a 2900 B.T.U.

heat radiation zone and grows a full variety of farm produce including corn, winter wheat, oats, barley, peas, and beans. The soil and terrain are particularly suited to dairy operations, being well drained and supplied with abundant water resources. The water table is only about fifteen feet below grade over most of the area and wells run full for the whole summer.

As a result of the Treaty of Paris in 1763, Canada became a British territory. In 1791, Quebec was divided into Upper and Lower Canada, each possessing its own legislative council and assembly, and in the same year, Augustus Jones received instructions to survey the land between the Trent and the Etobicoke for the purpose of establishing a series of townships. With the arrival in 1792 of a new Lieutenant Governor, Colonel John Graves Simcoe, the plan for the new province was to make it "the image and transcript of the British Constitution". By 1796, when the Governor had finished his term of office, he had incorporated towns, instituted English civil law, transformed the members of the legislative council into a landed gentry, and established the Church of England as a power in Upper Canada. Simcoe gave one seventh of all surveyed township land to the Church, as well as generous amounts to his civil servants and councillors. In Pickering alone, of the 74,660 acres which comprise the Township, 18,800 were in the hands of five people, three of whom were the Surveyor General and two members of his family. Much of the Township was taken up by military grants and absentee owners.

By 1800, Pickering was well on the road to development. As the settlers began arriving — Loyalist, English, Irish, Scottish and American — the Township underwent the gradual and astonishing metamorphosis from a forest into a community of people (who drank in 1850, when they were 6,000 in number, 80,000 gallons of whiskey produced by the Township's single distillery). Among the earliest arrivals were William Peak, a fur trader from Upper Canada, and Thomas Matthews, a Loyalist from the United States. Asa Danforth, an American, was contracted to build the road from King and Queen Streets in Toronto to Duffins Creek. Samuel Munger and Noadiah Woodruff were the first innkeepers, and

Timothy Rogers, a Quaker, in addition to building the first grist and saw mills on Duffins Creek, encouraged an entire community of Friends to settle in the Township. In 1808, there were some 180 settlers in the area and in 1811 the first by-law was passed at the Municipality's first town meeting to the effect that "fences be four feet and a half high and not more than five inches between rails". By 1850, almost half of the Township's land had been cleared of trees. In a book published in 1911, on the occasion of Pickering's one-hundredth anniversary, W.R. Wood described the evolution of the pioneer community: "Soon little 'clearance' surrounded the little log dwellings of the settlers, and season by season they widened till at length clearance joined clearance, then there came a time when the clearance was larger than the remaining 'bush', and the years hastened the time when only patches of forest are left to dot at wide intervals the landscape of the township." Trails through the forest became roads. Inns, general stores, and mills by the dozen became the focus of prosperous little communities like Pickering Village, Greenwood, Claremont, and Brougham — communities which lived up to the name whenever weddings, funerals, fairs, political speeches, and land-clearing or barn-raising bees provided the opportunity. In 1850, a Township census enumerated six grist mills, twenty-four saw mills, four carding mills, a tannery, and the distillery which, along with numerous private stills, helped to ameliorate the grinding life of the pioneers. Side by side there developed a temperance movement with a backbone of Friends and Mennonites. The forests were levelled and the land was cleared. Along with the forest went the salmon, prevented from spawning by the mill dams.

The Crimean War and the Reciprocity Treaty increased, in the early fifties, the price of wheat and the market for flour, lumber, wool, and hides turned out by Pickering industry. Frenchman's Bay was a busy harbour, and the first train ran from Toronto to Oshawa on August 25, 1856. Villages turned into towns and thought of becoming cities as the hum, even the roar, of industry replaced the stillness of the vanishing forest. Along with the mills, there were creameries and factories producing shingles, steam carriages, wagons, and cabinets; there were saddlers, coppers, tanners, and weavers; and in every town there were blacksmiths and carpenters, butchers and merchants, tailors and painters. No longer did the pioneers need a dozen skills. Brass bands were boasted by Brougham, Whitevale, and Claremont, and Pickering Village had six clergymen and a teacher.

Pickering appeared to be rushing towards the twentieth century, but by the seventies the boom ended as wheat declined as a commodity and the Township's lumber was exhausted. The milling industry almost vanished. Thousands of people left the Township for Toronto and points west and south, and towns reverted to villages, villages to hamlets. Dairy farming and apple orchards became new sources of income, as did hay and horse breeding (especially by the world-famous Graham brothers). Pickering Harbour was improved in the mid seventies with a lighthouse, an elevator, and a wharf, and for a time coal was successfully imported and barley was shipped. But the market failed and the village of Liverpool remained a village. Pickering Township had become and would remain a minor point of supply for the St. Lawrence Market in the rapidly growing City of Toronto. Not until 1952, after the Second World War had revived immigration and industry (especially the Ajax shell-filling plant), was the population equal to that of 1860.

The present population of Pickering Township numbers 31,738. Most of the large towns are in the south — Ajax, Pickering, and Bay Ridges. In the middle and upper portions are many towns ranging from 300 to 1500 residents — Claremont, Greenwood, Kinsdale, Whitevale, Green River, Altona, and Brougham. On its border are Markham with 13,000 people living on three square miles, Stouffville with 8,000 people on two square miles, and Unionville with 4,000 on one and one half square miles. These towns are completely surrounded by rural farmlands.

The government announcement to build an airport on 18,000 acres of land in Pickering and adjoining parts of Markham and Uxbridge Township will end forever a style of life which has evolved over 150 years. In addition, an adjacent city, "Cedarwood," which will have 200,000 people living on 25,000 acres (over 40 square miles), will take up the remaining open land in the south and create a solid mass of urbanization between Metro and Pickering. That is, almost half of the Township's 74,660 acres will vanish and the rest will be drastically affected.

The Ministry of Transport has said that 50 per cent of the land is owner-farmer occupied. The proposed site includes about 4,000 acres of the ill-fated Century City project, which the province of Ontario vetoed because it conficted with land reserved by the Toronto Centred Regional Plan for agriculture and recreation use. (Title to these lands is in dispute since Century City has failed to meet its mortgage payments.) Most of the Pickering area is owned locally, with some land having been bought for speculation. Higher than average taxes on farm lands have, to some extent, discouraged local farmers. But strict control of building permits have limited mushroom housing developments.

There are 126 working farms within the proposed site, with excellent farm buildings and 30 with substantial silos. Sales of seed and feed from the Co-operative have not declined and the purchases of grain (oats, wheat, and corn) have been increasing. Farm equipment depots continue to flourish. There are numerous 4-H members. Some non-resident owners have provided rental opportunities to local farmers, allowing them to increase the size of their operations and productivity.

A modest estimate of gross production from the 18,000 acres, based on 50 bushels of wheat per acre at $1.70 per bushel, is $1,530,000.00 per year. If devoted to dairying the gross revenue would exceed $2,500,000.00. When the 25,000 acre Cedarwood development is added to the 18,000 acre airport, there will be an agricultural loss exceeding five million dollars per annum. Within ten years of a complete airport, all land between Agincourt, Markham, and Unionville will be developed. Two new superhighways will lead to the airport, one cutting east-west through North York, Markham, and Pickering. The second, an extension of the Gardiner, will bisect Scarborough. In addition all existing main roads and highways will be widened and developed. It is estimated there will be 200,000 people to the east of Markham, at least 200,000 to the south, and

200,000 in Cedarwood itself.

As it now exists, Pickering is a "historic community". Much of its past, and that of Canada's, can still be seen. Each community has its museum or famous landmark. One of the earliest inns, built by George Post in 1815, is still standing on Kingston Road. The Bently Home in Brougham with its widows walk is known to all. The numerous square-cut granite stone farmhouses in which have lived Reesors, Widemans, Annis, McBradys, Burkholders, and Stovers may still be seen behind the pine windbreaks. Some of the visual history has been destroyed by fire which has changed the character of the countryside; fire has also claimed much of the forest, innumerable mills, and buildings like Pickering College, which succeeded the Quaker's Seminary in 1877 and burned down in 1905. Some of the famous community sons have not been forgotten: T. Burton who opened a store in Greenwood and fathered the founder of the Robert Simpson Company, C.L. Burton; and John G. Diefenbaker, who on May 28, 1957, visited Greenwood Public School, his first place of learning, where his father, Mr. W.T. Diefenbaker, once taught. Concluding his remarks, Mr. Diefenbaker claimed that, "Father and I both agreed, on our visit here in 1924, that the five years spent here around the turn of the century represented some of the happiest days of our lives."

The great majority of residents of the airport area share this sentiment. Residents who are the grandchildren of the original settlers. Residents who represent the new pioneers who have left the city to choose a new way of life; who fight traffic and snowstorms; who give up the attractions of the big city; who may live on hobby farms or real farms, in communes or cottages, in small towns or deserted sideroads. All are united in a determination to live out their lives and raise their families in Pickering.

2. The Need

Milton Mowbray settled back in his seat on the 8:50 and be-
gan to read the morning paper. His seatmates began the usual
activities that filled out the time taken in the three-quarter-
hour trip from Claremont to Union Station. Bridge, talk,
reading, or sleeping. Mowbray eased a legal brief from his
attaché case and began to study a presentation to be made
next week. Occasionally he glanced out the window at the
landscape. The train passed Lots 7 and 8, the sixth-concession
Pickering where his great grandfather, Ralph, had first settled.
He had come to Pickering from Ireland in 1833, carrying the
first logging chains and axes from little York. The log cabin
they had built had disappeared to be replaced by a red brick
Ontario farm house.

His grandson Ralph R. Mowbray had been Reeve of Picker-
ing in 1911 and had served the municipality in township and
county councils for eighteen years. He had been the Liberal
candidate for the federal riding in 1911. And now Milton was
riding the dayliner to Toronto. When he returned home that
night he would go to the meeting at Melody Farm.

Lengthy consideration of the need for a second major airport
in southern Ontario logically and practically preceded the
question of its site. By 1966, aircraft movement at Malton
(Toronto I) had increased from ten per day in 1938 to over

two hundred. To facilitate phenomenal growth in the Toronto region in 1968 the airport was expanded from its initial 1400 acres to 4200, and facilities were established to accommodate jet passenger aircraft. The Malton Master Plan (1967) was a detailed study by John B. Parkin Associates and commissioned by the Federal Ministry of Transport of the long-range growth of air traffic in the Toronto region.

The Plan predicted the continued growth of air traffic in the seventies and eighties, recommended the acquisition of large quantities of adjacent lands for more runways and terminal buildings, outlined the need for an increase of road lanes and access routes to and from the airport, and warned that additional air activity would result in increased noise factor and greater exposure to flight operations.

In the summer of 1968 the federal government announced the intention to expand Malton as recommended. Mr. Paul Hellyer, Minister of Transport at the time, remarked that the proposed expansion would solve Metropolitan Toronto's transportation problems for twenty-five years. The response of the residents of the area was shock, leading to an organized community protest. Hellyer and other representatives were dismayed by the response. On closer examination of the figures revealing how many residents would be affected, it was discovered a miscalculation had been made in the affected noise zones and that a larger number of residents were to be affected than had been anticipated. In addition the proposed ground expansion was a threat to potential building lots which could be developed in the future. A strong citizens' organization, SANA, sprang up and held a series of meetings protesting the expansion. About seven thousand members were involved. These included some real-estate developers and municipal members.

The result of this protest was overkill. While the majority of residents felt they could get along with a modest expansion at Malton, as long as certain modifications were made in the flight procedures and in reality welcomed further employment opportunities which would be offered with an expanded airport, the federal government took the objection as a solid vote against *any* expansion. Ottawa decided not to proceed with the full expansion of Malton, but to establish a joint federal-provincial committee to recommend a comprehensive aviation system for southern Ontario. As an interim measure, a new passenger terminal was to be built and extensions effected to the runway and taxiway system.

Malton's potential was subjected to further examinations, and it was decided that it would continue to play a crucial role in any new plan. It was pointed out that new types of aircraft were quieter even though they were larger. The Boeing 747, Lockhead 1011, and McDonnell Douglas DC-10 had double the seats and less noise than the Boeing 707 or the McDonnell Douglas DC-8. Even more significant was the advanced development of short take-off and landing aircraft (STOL). With reduced noise factor these would be ideal for short distances and intercity travel. In the opinion of the experts Malton would continue to handle over twelve million passengers each year.

The necessity for a new airport was on the basis of increased noise and social disruption, which would occur with the expected increase in aircraft if Malton remained a sole airport for the Toronto region. In the early stages of decision-making, this was the only consideration.

What were the bases of the air passenger forecast which indicated the need for a new airport?

"Air passenger forecasting is one of the lesser sophisticated varieties of forecasting in use today," stated the *Regional Impact of a New International Airport for Toronto* (prepared by the Ontario Department of Treasury and Economics and completed in March of 1970). It continued:

Although factors such as price reduction rates, population projections, and increased propensity to travel have been included in various forecast methodologies, many unknowns have yet to be resolved. For instance: "At what rate will our leisure time increase? Will it be used for more travel? What proportion of travel will be by air? What will be the effect of larger and faster aircraft? Will new highspeed ground transportation be a substitute? These are only a few of the pertinent questions that cannot currently be answered but yet each can gravely affect future airline patronage.[1]

The questions raised in the paragraph are clearly pertinent and the authors demonstrated this through reference to another "travel industry": "When it was in a comparable development phase, the automobile industry had increasingly high average annual consumption rates. If these past acceleration rates held true the current ownership rate would be tremendously higher than it presently is. In per capita terms, car ownership has tended to level off. . . ."

The analogy is then made more explicit — but still kept simple: "If the high average air traffic growth rates of the recent past are applied in a straight-line manner, we would soon be forecasting scores of trips per person annually. Obviously, this will not be the case: the profile of the forecast curve will tend to resemble a logistics curve much as has happened with automobile ownership." Few would want to argue with such reasoning; opposing natural forces are historically noted for keeping straight-line. Unfortunately, however, such established patterns are not recognized in the Ministry of Transport.

"Trend lines approximating those of the past 15 to 20 year period are currently being used, with no indication of a levelling off in the next 30 years. After 1985, the average annual rate of air passenger growth is expected by M.O.T. to be 13% and continue to at least the Year 2000."[2] A failure in thought is obvious here, one that cannot be minimized or blamed on the planners in the Department of Treasury and Economics. The accompanying table draws several interesting conclusions.

In both of their projections, DOT has used an annual increment of 8.8 percent to 1985, yielding 18.9 million passengers. From that time on, growth is projected to increase at an ever faster rate — 12 percent annually — such that by Year 2000 there would be 96.4 million passengers accommodated yearly by both Malton and Toronto II. Even the most "pessimistic" DOT view foresees at least a continuation of the 8 percent rate, giving 60.0 million passengers by Year 2000.

"In terms of today's totals (1965), this 96 million would represent the present combined activity of all three New York airports, Chicago's O'Hare, Los Angeles, Atlanta, San Francisco, Washington's National, Miami, Boston, Dallas — Ft. Worth, Detroit, Kansas City, and Seattle-Taconia."[3] To

11

Department of Transport Alternate Forecasts of Air Passenger Movements for Toronto Region Airports

(Millions of passengers)

	Year	(1) (a)	(b)	(2)
Past (Malton only)	1967	3.3	3.3	
	1968	4.5	4.5	
Future	1970	5.3	5.3	
Earliest possible opening	1975	8.1	8.1	
	1980	3.6		
		8.8	12.4	
	1985	5.4		
		13.5	18.9	18.9
	1990	8.7		
		23.8	32.5	27.8
	1995	14.0		
		41.9	55.9	40.8
	2000	22.55		
		78.9	96.4	60.0

NOTES: Column 1(a) is subdivided by airport — the top figure for each year representing Malton, the bottom Toronto II (Pickering).

(1) is based on:

i. an 8.8 per cent average annual increase to 1985.

ii. a 10 per cent average annual increase from 1985 to 2000 for Malton.

iii. a 12 per cent average annual increase from 1985 to 2000 for Toronto II.

(2) is based on:

i. an 8.8 per cent average annual increase to 1985.

ii. an 8 per cent average annual increase to 2000.

gain another perspective, compare this 96 million to the 400 million passengers forecast for the entire United States in 1979 (Federal Aviation Administration).[4]

Gerald Hodge, the writer of the report ended up by suggesting that the truth most likely lay between the thirty million which he foresaw and the ninety-six million, seen by the Department of Transport. He suggested that the most likely prediction might be somewhere in the middle of the two expectations. This splitting of the difference characterizes many of the calculations dealing with expected loads.

Limits to Growth reflects much of the same sentiment used in this type of forecasting. It argues as follows:

The principal defect of the industrial way of life with its ethos of expansion is that it is not sustainable. Its termination within the lifetime of someone born today is inevitable — unless it continues to be sustained for a while longer by an entrenched minority at the cost of imposing great suffering on the rest of mankind. We can be certain, however, that sooner or later it will end. . . .[5]

The "planners" of the Department of Transport seem more inclined to obey figures from the recent past than to shape a future with care.

At times the government's figures do not even add to the same sums twice. For example, "Aviation in Canada — 1971", predicts a passenger volume of twenty-one million at Toronto by 1990 (not including charter flights). Accompanying the announcement of the new airport at Pickering, the figure had jumped to 33 million.[6]

Passenger Handling Capacity

The ability of any airport to handle passengers depends upon the ground facilities available. Terminals either at the airport or remote may be the deciding factor that permits a relatively small airport to handle a large number of aircraft movements. At Heathrow in London, check-in facilities are provided downtown and the passengers go directly to the embarkation gate by bus. In Tokyo a monorail system quickly whips the passenger from Haneda to downtown Tokyo. Brussels permits the passenger to check in at one of several terminals and be taken to the airport by a high-speed electric train system.

Any new site in Ontario would have to guarantee the traveller rapid access to the city. This is particularly so if Malton is not to continue as the main airport. A remarkable number of people (some 84 percent of passengers embarking and disembarking) move to and from the airport by automobile transport at the present time. This compares with approximately 40 per cent at Kennedy in New York City.

Part of the disaffection with Malton is its inability to sustain a greatly increased number of people driving to the airport. Unless massive road arrangements are made or rapid-speed ground transport is provided, its future is limited. (It is realized that automobile transport also adds to the pollution and noise problems around the airport.) Ground facilities to properly handle passengers and baggage must also be provided.

Aircraft Movements

One of the main factors that indicated Malton was not adequate for the future was the number of passengers who would take off in the 1990s. Early government documents stress this factor. However, there was rapid centring of criticism on this aspect with the assertion that aircraft movements, not passenger movements, must be the recognizable measure of an airport's capacity.

Aircraft movement depends on many factors. Big loads (in peak hours when it is most convenient for businessmen to travel) in the period from eight to ten in the morning and four to six in the afternoon makes the airport seem much busier than it actually is.

The mix of aircraft — a small number of seats in the DC-8 compared with the 380 of a 747 — may make considerable difference in the number of aircraft movements.

Load factor — the number of occupied seats — is an important consideration. Most commercial flights operate with a load factor of approximately 46 per cent. This means that many seats are unoccupied. However, the number of aircraft movements are not reduced. Charter aircraft or air-bus schedules guarantee a much higher load factor with a resultant decrease of aircraft movement.

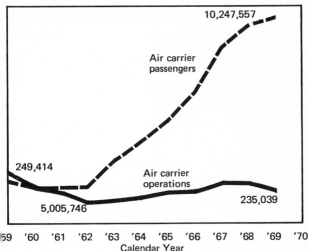

SOURCE: Federal Aviation Authority, *Statistical Handbook of Aviation.*

NOTE: A remarkable demonstration of the effect of better load factor in the movement of passengers may be seen from the Washington airport. Several years ago it was decided that Washington National Airport could not continue to grow beyond four million passengers. Accordingly the John Foster Dulles International Airport was built well outside the city. It remains under-utilized as the passengers prefer to use the downtown airport because of convenience. This graph shows the phenomenal rise of passengers flying into and out of the airport with no increase in the number of aircraft movements.

In 1971, aircraft movements at Malton were lower than in 1970 and only 6 per cent higher than in 1967. The 1970 airport study commissioned by the Ministry of Transport indicated that the regular scheduled and charter movements for 1976 *will be less by 6½ per cent than actual 1971 movements* (see table 1). In 1971 there were 213,876

Table 1
1970 Actual Movements and Ministry of Transport Projections 1976-2000
Projections from 1970 Ministry of Transport report

Annual Movements	1971 actual	1976	1981	1985	1990	2000
Scheduled						
Domestic	69,478	52,480	64,260	74,800	---	---
Transborder	40,253	44,020	53,600	60,740	---	---
Other international	6,255	10,240	14,080	18,260	---	---
Total	115,986	106,740	131,940	153,800	---	---
Charter	5,418	6,641	9,379	12,062	---	---
Total annual aircraft movements	121,404	113,381	141,319	165,862	204,000	345,700

Table 2
Total Aircraft Movements by Class of Operation
Toronto International Airport – 1971

Itinerant movements (non-local)	Number	Percentage of Total
Regular scheduled	115,986	54.2%
Charter	5,418	2.5%
Other commercial	16,954	7.9%
Private	35,710	16.6%
Government	2,916	1.3%
Local	22,136	10.0%
Simulated approaches	14,756	6.9%

movements at Malton. *Only 121,404 or 56 per cent of all movements were regular scheduled or chartered movements* (see table 2). If runway capacity ever does become a problem at Malton, most of the local, general aviation (private and other commercial) movements can be directed to other smaller airports. Even if a new airport had to be built at some point in the future to handle these small aircraft, it would require a fraction of Malton's present runway capacity strength and size.

Aviation consultants state that without even adding a runway, Malton can in future handle over 355,000 movements. The 1970 study by the Ministry of Transport projected 165,862 regular schedules and charter movements in 1985 and 204,000 in 1990. This suggests that even if most private and small aircraft are not diverted, Malton can handle aircraft movements until 1985-1990 without adding a runway. Even if the above projections prove to be low, the most that would happen is that private and small aircraft would have to be removed from Malton earlier.

Improved air traffic control systems will have a substantial effect on increasing an airport's capacity even further. A comprehensive study of the technology of air-traffic control has been made in the United States by the Air Traffic Control Committee of the Department of Transportation. This study indicates that even with present technology, airport capacity can be doubled. Some of the improvements possible involve reducing runway separation, the use of dual-lane runways (one for take off, one for landing), and the reduction of minimum separation between aircraft on approach.

There are no practical technological limits to aircraft size. The size of existing commercial aircraft is limited by expected passenger loads rather than technology. If landing fees are changed to take into account the fact that huge capital expenditures for new airports are caused by increased movements at existing facilities then the use of even larger aircraft would be encouraged.

Cost-related scheduling and pricing will also have an effect on airport capacity. If, for example, landing fees were increased at peak periods during the day, prices could reflect this, thereby encouraging people to travel at off-peak hours.

Note the recent fare schedule proposed by Canadian Pacific which suggests this.

Air constraints on an airport's ability to handle its load include apron and parking facilities. These demand additional areas to the runways and terminals. Fortunately these were not a major consideration at Malton, as there was a large amount of industrial land which could be used for these purposes, including aircraft-manufacturing installations which no longer required access to the airfield.

With these considerations which would be operative in searching for a new site, it is interesting to compare Malton's potential against the new sites. While it was not mentioned in the criteria, an overall consideration for siting a new airport is the effects on the surrounding countryside and residents.

The Effects of Noise on Malton Residents

In one of the brochures released by Mr. Jamieson on April 26th, it was stated that if Malton were physically expanded with a runway alignment as envisaged in the 1967 plant, 70,000 people would be affected. But other government reports show there is no need to physically expand Malton *or even add a runway*. Therefore, the figure of 70,000 is far above the actual number of people who would be affected if Malton continued to be Toronto's only airport into the foreseeable future.

In comparing the advantages and disadvantages of opening a new airport anywhere from 1976-85, the September 1970 report of the Ministry of Transport mentioned that one factor which favoured an early opening of a second airport was the aircraft noise reduction around Malton. However, they went on to state that "the amount of reduced noise is expected to apply to only about 7,800 residents and involves only minor reductions on the noise level to those individuals (estimated to be 5 CNR* or the assumed traffic split)."[7] This is a far cry from 70,000 people. How much further could it be

*Composite Noise Rating — a mathematical equation which considers noise levels, frequency of exposure, and type of noise, and measures these to five (an index number or rating).

18

educed if some of the actions being planned for New York were applied at Malton?

Modern aircraft engines are getting quieter. Our own Ministry of Transport has given us no estimate of how the trend towards quieter aircraft affects Malton residents. However, a detailed study by the National Academy of Sciences and the National Academy of Engineering on Kennedy airport published in 1971 stated that "high bypass turbo fans such as are presently being installed in the B-747, DC-10 and L-1011 will *yield a net noise reduction on local communities.* This will occur in spite of an increase by 1980 of 27 per cent in aircraft movements . . . or 150% in passenger movements."[8]

Since further reference will be made to the Kennedy Airport study, a few comments should be made about it. In December of 1969 the Port of New York Authority (PONYA) approached the Environmental Studies Board (a joint board of the National Academy of Sciences and the National Academy of Engineering) to study the impact of runway extension at Kennedy Airport.

The study was multi-disciplinary, involving twenty-five investigators from the physical and biological sciences, engineering, the social and behavioral sciences, and the law. It is a comprehensive and objective study and is of great importance to airport planners all over the world.

The Kennedy study also points out that:

current engine technology could yield a further reduction in noise level of 10 EPN db* with some penalty on direct operating cost. It appears that the added cost should not exceed 10% on the ticket price and would probably be much less. Such "quiet" engines could be ready for installation on new aircraft by 1975, provided a firm decision for implementation is made soon. In the interim a substantial reduction in noise from the present aircraft fleet can be had at minor cost by means of a nacelle-retrofit program. This program could be complete by 1975.[9]

The Kennedy report points out that when existing aircraft are modified and when 1970 technology aircraft like the B-747, DC-10, L-1011 are made 10 EPN db quieter, the

*The effective perceived noise measured in decibels.

number of people around Kennedy Airport exposed to excessive noise *could be reduced by a factor of 10—from about 500,000 to 45,000*. Obviously a similar benefit available to residents around Malton. And the 1980s and '90s will bring further technological advances in the design of quieter engines.

What is the Ministry of Transport doing to reduce noise around Malton and other airports in Canada? Why does it not make attempts to cure the disease rather than treating the symptom. Where are the results of the Ministry of Transport's detailed studies on the possibility of reducing aircraft noise?

On what basis does the Ministry of Transport say in its recently published brochure on the Development Plan for Malton that "the reduced rate of growth in flights and the quieter engines will limit the spread of noise during the seventies", and go on to say that "the daily lives of many people around Malton would be increasingly disturbed beyond the 1970s". Let us have the facts supporting these statements. The Kennedy report states that the noise situation can be greatly improved without adding another airport even though passenger volumes are forecasted to increase at about the same rate as ours. The report claims that the trend towards quieter engines will increase rather than lessen in the future. The Port of New York Authority is taking positive steps now to ensure that this is the case. What is different about the Malton situation?

User Convenience

The time and cost taken for a passenger to get to his airplane is called user convenience. Any new airport in Pickering or anywhere else must equal or better Malton's facilities. Not only is Malton at the region's demographic centre, but studies have shown that far more users of Malton originate from the west than from the east. Malton is ideally situated to accommodate this western bias as far as Hamilton.

In their initial statements on March 2nd, both Mr. McKeough and Mr. Jamieson stressed that they had to keep two publics in mind. The one group includes those affected y a new airport. The second and larger group involves the airport users.

Given the government figure of a shift of population to the east and even with the possibility that the planned south-western Ontario system of airports might divert some Malton traffic, the needs of the user are best served by having one airport at Malton. Estimates are that users east of Yonge street would not be more than 5 million passengers by 1990 (letter from Kates Peat Marwick & Co. to D.R. Hemming, September 30, 1970). Besides the question of location, there are the additional complications created by the needs of transferring passengers between one airport and the other, complications which would not exist with a one airport system.

Costs

The cost of an airport includes initial ground cost, building and developments, and user cost. In addition, negative costs such as land compensation, environmental damage, and social disruption must be included.

Continued utilization of Malton is a very much cheaper solution than building a second airport. In its September 1970 report the Ministry of Transport estimated, after taking into account direct and indirect user costs as well as capital and operating costs over the twenty-year period, 1980-2000, that a new airport would cost anywhere between just under $5 billion and $6.4 billion depending on the site chosen. Even if the proposed airport at Pickering as scaled down were cheaper, we would still be talking of between 4 and 5 billion dollars. Of this amount over half is related to user costs, and a part of this would be incurred at Malton at any rate. However, since Malton is situated at the region's demographic centre, user costs would be very much less than at any other site.

Although we have not at this point in time a detailed cost-benefit analysis comparing continued use of Malton until the year 2000 with the opening of another airport in 1980, it could be shown, on the basis of the 1970 study, that the difference would be somewhere between 1½ to 3 billion

21

dollars, even after incurring considerable expenditure o
expanding Malton's passenger-handling capacity.

Even if a new airport were needed at some point in tim
(such as 1990), every year that construction is delayed resul
in a considerable saving to the Canadian taxpayer.

Other Factors

Short take-off and landing (STOL) and vertical take-off an
landing (VTOL) aircraft, operating from close-in fields, are i
an advanced stage of development and would not only reduc
passenger flow but also aircraft movements of the long
runway airports. Another possibility, already in existence bu
not in this country, is the high-speed train; it offers a no
unattractive travel proposition over stages of up to 300 miles

The desirability of such innovations should be clear to
government supposedly pledged to "anticipating furthe
advances in technology . . . especially in terms of the quality
of our environment . . .".[10] Yet they are almost totally
ignored in the published planning reports.

A writer for *The Toronto Star* has pointed out that "the
same Department of Transport experts who now tell us that
second airport is imperative, made just as good a case in 196٤
for an expanded Malton being capable of handling an?
increase that might take place during this century."[11] The
remark is useful for crystallizing the amount of manipulatio٦
that surrounds the government's explanations. However, on
case should be better than the other!

Data and ideas have been presented here to argue the need
for a single airport—in this case an airport described as "on
of the best in the world." "Three senior pilots," as the *Star*
writer observed, "two of them spokesmen for the Canadian
Air Line Pilots Association have on separate occasions pub
licly damned two-airport plans as a waste of the taxpayers'
money." In the case of the proposed Toronto II at Pickering.
"waste" will be seen shortly to include important quantities
of rich farm land, of recreational and conservational spaces,
of wildlife and water, as well as taxpayers' money.

The credibility of statements made by federal Transport

finister Don Jamieson and Darcy McKeough, then Minister
f Municipal Affairs, was challenged on June 27th, 1972, by
lark Muirhead, an Uxbridge (Ontario) Councillor and Vice-
hairman of the People or Planes technical committee.

t's ridiculous that the Minister bases his 1972 statements on an
bsolete 1967 study. He appears to use the handiest information to
uit the occasion, and it apparently doesn't matter if one study has
een negated by another if he feels it will sway his audience on the side
f the second airport development.

This 1970 plan proposed that $70 million be set aside to com-
ensate present residents living in noise zones around Malton. Despite
his, the cost of utilizing Malton was calculated to be $1.1 billion less
xpensive than that for expropriating and developing a second
nternational airport in Toronto.

The new plan, you'll notice, does not allow compensation for
ither the present Malton residents, or the 28,000 people which
overnment studies show will be adversely affected by airport opera-
ions at the Pickering site.

3. The Choice

Jane Buckles watched her husband, Brian, pull out of the drive. The Toyota had bucked against the snow which had been laid across the driveway by the plow. The sun was barely shining through the grey overcast, and it looked like a cold day.

The house was beginning to warm up as the furnace churned away. The pine sideboard and kitchen table looked warm but felt cold to the touch as Jane cleared away the breakfast dishes. Kelly, her daughter, was beginning to play with her dolls in front of the burned-out fireplace from last night.

By eleven o'clock the telephone was ringing. The news of the airport, the expropriation, the outrage, and the dismay all piled over the receiver as many friends in the area pooled their feelings.

After four years of struggling to rebuild an old farmhouse, a new way of life in this old farm, the government was going to take it away. After years of looking forward to peace and quiet away from the city rackets and away from Brian's computing pressures, the government had decided to interfere. Just when the gardens were beginning to show promise, the house was beginning to be comfortable, and the new friends in the neighbourhood were becoming enjoyable.

And why? Was there a real reason to build a new air-

ort? To cut down that beautiful maple bush? To kill the
ed-shouldered hawk who was cruising over last summer's
ornfield?

Surely there could be a better use for this last bit
f land that offered the Metro worker a chance to pull him-
elf together, a chance to recreate his soul.

She thought of the many friends who came out on the week-
nds, bringing their children, picnicking under the gnarled
pple trees down by the old well. The conversations they
ad had. "Your country estate — your acres — your fief-
lom." How they had argued about the moral right for an
wner to possess a piece of heaven while many townspeople
ere denied entry by fence and gate.

She remembered Brian saying he could see that some day
he government would have to set aside the land in this
rea for the citizens of Metro, and to that he would have
o graciously bow recognizing that in the long run the
arth belonged to all.

"But to take this land for an airport is a crime,"
he said into the telephone, as the fourth neighbour was
dissolving in tears of frustration as she recounted what
he radio had told her. "A crime against the land — and
gainst my family."

Jane Buckles prepared for the meeting that was to be
held that evening.

Under the terms of the British North America Act, the
selection and regulation of airports is a federal responsibility.
However, the impact of any federal decision "rests heavily on
areas well within the provinces' concern". The Ontario
government's involvement in the decision to build a second
international airport in the Toronto region is no secret. The
province was committed to the provision of adequate facilities to supplement or replace those at Malton as well as to
ensure that any new development would fit into the Toronto
Centred Region *Design for Development.* Hence the decision
of March 2nd to set up a system of airports for the Toronto

25

region was reached after a complex series of negotiations by the provincial and federal governments.

From the federal viewpoint the predominant problem was noise. It was noise that had stopped Hellyer in his ambition to expand Malton. It was noise that marked the move to some other area in order to placate the voter in Etobicoke. No matter what studies were done by top-notch firms, unless the noise could be reduced, the studies were not pertinent.

Because of the inability to proceed with Malton, it was decided by December 1968 to undertake examination of other alternatives. However, before that a further report was received which discussed a limited expansion of Malton requiring only an additional 1,000 acres and provision for growth only to 1985. The report concluded:

To satisfy the passenger, cargo and aircraft forecasts, early and positive action to increase capacity is demanded. The Department and Consultants are in agreement that expansion of the Toronto International Airport is the most economic and viable course of action subject to land availability, compatible land use and an adequate ground transportation system. . . .

Should this approach prove inconsistent with Provincial or Municipal Long Range Plans other and more costly alternatives will have to be explored.[1]

This report was never implemented.

Assured that Malton would not be expanded, the Ontario government introduced land-use contracts in the noise area to ensure growth compatible with flight operations. In announcing the contracts, Darcy McKeough, then Minister of Municipal Affairs, stated that they represented "the first comprehensive attempt by any jurisdiction in North America to ensure that the utilization of land in the vicinity of an airport would be compatible with the high noise levels generated by aircraft operations".

By early 1969, the Ministry of Transport discovered that it had no recourse but to find a "more costly alternative". It organized the Toronto Airports Planning Team to determine the location of a site for a second airport to serve Toronto. Some of the federal government's major concerns were:
• To provide the most efficient possible airport system to the southern Ontario region.

To locate the new international airport where it can safely and conveniently best serve the travelling public.

• To protect the public from adverse influences; i.e., noise, pollution, etc.

• To minimize the costs and maximize the financial benefits of the new airport.

• To locate the airport in an area where it will have the best possible impact on the growth of the southern Ontario economy.

Finally, the airport should be located where it will have an effect upon the sound and orderly planning (and become an integral part) of the development of the southern Ontario region.[2]

Given these criteria the Planning Team carried out preliminary investigations of the implications of a new Toronto airport. An interim report dated May 1969 concluded that a new airport was urgently needed to serve Toronto region. By mid 1969, a federal-provincial task force was set up to seek an alternate site. The federal team identified fifty-nine sites within a fifty-mile radius of Toronto, all falling within four broad zones—Toronto north (including northeast), west (including southwest), northwest, and east. The original criteria called for a six-runway airport which would be a major factor in reducing the load on Malton use in the coming years. This criterion quickly ruled out many of the fifty-nine sites. It also escalated costs to an unacceptable level. (By dint of rethinking, the criterion was lowered to four runways.) Using the criteria listed above federal and provincial officials set about reducing the list to a few sites. The four sites received as most favourable were Lake Simcoe, Lake Scugog, Campbellville, and Orangeville. As part of the overall inquiry, the Ontario government commissioned the study "Regional Impact of a New International Airport For Toronto" (March 1970). The Hodge Report (named after its author Gerald Hodge) emphasized that "the decision to locate the new international airport for Toronto should be made with regard to the *impact* of the facility on economic development and structure of the region and its affected areas"[3]. Other points of significance include the following:

- When Toronto II does begin operation it will have to accommodate by 1990 a flow of passengers five times Malton's present total, 20 million passengers annually (Malton now handles 7 million).
- Of the four sites chosen Orangeville and Lake Scugog are favoured.
- The four sites considered are located at the outer extent of the present "commutershed". The establishment of the new airport will mean the establishment of a "growth centre" on the periphery between the Toronto and adjacent regions.

The Hodge Report as well as three studies commissioned by the federal government were summarized in the provincial document "Submission to the Government of Canada In Respect of the Location of The Second International Airport For the Toronto Region" (April 1970). The submissions were: Lake Simcoe would prove the most costly of the four sites—the other three presented no significant difference . . . from the point of view of cost. The Lake Scugog site conforms extremely well to the long-term development concept of the region. Its main disadvantage is that the passenger markets are west of Toronto, and the problem of accessibility to the new airport would be increased. This site like Orangeville and Campbellville presents little or no problems from an environmental and ecological point of view. Lake Simcoe would present "significant destructive influences" and would be "harmful to the recreational potential of the Toronto region". The report concluded that the operative trade-off in the evaluation process is the importance assigned to cost benefits.

Choice requires a policy decision. From late 1969 to mid 1970 federal-provincial discussions intensified. To make the best possible choice, the Ministry of Transport set up in 1970 an Advisory Committee composed of its officials as well as a number of consultants. Two of the more prominent names were Hans Blumenfeld and Phil Beinhacker, the former an urbanologist on the faculty of the University of Toronto and the latter a city planner and architect with Kates Peat Marwick & Co. Beinhacker's career has been linked to the Ministry of Transport. In 1967-70, he served the government

28

n many capacities on the Ste. Scholastique Airport. He was consultant, researcher, and project manager. In May 1970, Mr. Beinhacker was commissioned to review the progress of the planning team. With a magnificent disregard for his predecessors, his main recommendations were:

• The new airport was unnecessary and public demand "will likely be exerted for continued services through Malton".
• The costs to develop a new Toronto International Airport are indeed very great—the aggregate capital costs will be at least twice those for Montreal. Since airport and adjacent land is costly, the Federal and Provincial Governments should set up a land bank.[4]

He added a series of reports that examined many possible alternate strategies and that included

• Expand Malton and compensate residents by buying out those who objected to noise.
• A multiple airport system with Malton a major facility.
• A multiple airport system including Malton, Hamilton, east and north airports with connecting links.
• A giant integration of aviation and surface travel with Eastern Canada.
• A completely new Toronto International Airport with an integrated urban transportation system.

Each of these strategies held many attractions but in the end he plumped for an expansion of Malton.

However, a report goes on to say that "It is generally agreed and decided by *the Minister* that Malton alone is not saleable and that the plan must include provision of a new airport to maintain flexibility."

At this stage another dimension was added to the factors which indicated the need for a second airport—flexibility.

The report by Blumenfeld was even more direct. After considering various ways of making Malton more effective, particularly with recommendation for mini-terminals and a better ground-transport system to reduce the number of people who went to Malton to wave good-bye to their relatives, he suggested that if the government was serious in its desire to repair the damage at Malton, it should close Malton down. Cost benefits were given on the basis of selling the Malton land for other real-estate businesses, thereby compensating local airport business concerns for loss of revenue and providing the cost necessary to build a new airport. This airport was to be located in an area where there would be no problem in the future of noise pollution.

These two consultants displayed a keen grasp of the economics of airport siting. In addition, Mr. Beinhacker showed considerable awareness of business psychology. In discussing "Flexibility" he realized that it would be difficult to sell this to the public. In order to manage this problem he suggested

the plan can provide all the necessary flexibility so long as the roles of the various airports are not determined now but are left to be decided as technology evolves and as the various urban areas and air-traffic markets develop. This point was appreciated by the Minister who agreed that, in the public dialogue, no definitions of role should be described. This is a vital aspect of the strategic plan and the entire Federal negotiation position. Its importance can't be minimized. Accordingly it has been agreed that the technical report on the alternatives to be made public should propose the sites under a continuum of roles for the new airport, from inter-continental charters and some scheduled activity up to the new airport accommodating most of the traffic. The Cabinet document that we are preparing as part of our third strategic assignment would similarly emphasize this point.[5]

He was also aware of the problems associated with the acquisition and protection of a large area of land in the Toronto Centred Region. He stated:

The experience of the new Montreal International Airport will provide a useful precedent for measuring and anticipating this disruption. Such disruption will be generally a function of a number of people resident on the land and the number and types of communities affected. It was worth noting that, in the case of Montreal, some ten thousand people had been affected and while this represents social problems of concern, this was anticipated and can be dealt with effectively. An open and proper approach to information dissemination, effective management and decision making in the designated community and the attention, fair and understanding attitude towards the people affected, can reduce problems to a manageable level.

30

Meanwhile in mid 1970 the Ontario government had reservations about some of the proposed sites. In its plan *Design for Development: The Toronto Centred Region* the government called for measures to encourage development to the east of Toronto. The plan also provided for a green belt around an urban core wherein there would be easy access to recreational areas, clean air, clean water, etc. Writing in an *Appendix to Design for Development* in August 1971, the Minister of Municipal Affairs stated, "our policy is to maintain land use essentially in the present form, that is mainly agricultural, recreational and open space".

This statement appeared six months before the announcement of the Pickering Airport and Cedarwood City proposals. The retention of "identifiable communities" and green belt had earlier been spelled out by Mr. McNaughton, then Provincial Treasurer:

Some of our best land is being lost to speculation and taken prematurely from agricultural uses ... Some of our scenic areas are being developed with little regard to the need for public access and conservation for future generations.

On the same day, May 5, 1970, the premier of the province, Mr. John Robarts, in presenting *Design for Development*, stated:

Each generation leaves upon the land the marks of its creativity. More than ever before, it is important that the current generation think and act positively and wisely. We are thinking not only of people and governments, but also of the old, the young, and of generations of the future.

Mr. Robarts also made a number of important points concerning the regional plan:

We must anticipate for their advances in technology, increases in wealth and changes in the aspirations and expectations of our people, especially in terms of the quality of our people, especially in terms of the quality of our environment, higher standards of community life and more readily available recreational facilities.

31

At this stage the federal government still thought in terms of a single airport. The provincial government favoured an eastern site. But there were second thoughts about the four sites and the province undertook yet another internal review on the proposed expansion of Malton. The examination of the capabilities of the present facilities showed:[6]

• The present facility could be expanded to accommodate all air traffic expected to the year 2000.
• Ground transportation could not handle the traffic generated by such an airport unless a change was made in the methods of handling passengers to and from the airport. A system of mini-terminals could be used.
• Expanding Malton would cost "35 to 65% below the cost levels associated with the external sites". The savings in primary capital costs alone are 400 million dollars."
• The proposal to expand existing facilities "will not completely disrupt" the regional development concept for the Toronto Centred region.
• Finally the report concluded that "the political history of the expansion of this site is such as to suggest that further encroachment on urban land, further increases in noise and air pollution and further risk of safety hazards is socially unacceptable in this area."

To overcome "socially unacceptable" difficulties the report advocated stringent technical controls to prevent the further spread of noise and air pollution as well as "strong control of servicing and subdivision approvals"[7] to keep population down.

About the same time that Ontario published its study, the federal government's *Technical Report* (Sept. 15th) on site evaluations was published. The site team favoured Campbellville — between Guelph and Milton — as the least expensive, rating Lake Scugog and Lake Simcoe third and fourth respectively. Paralleling the Technical Report, Beinhacker undertook a strategic planning assignment in which he concluded that:

The existing airport at Malton is well located to serve the present and future air travellers of the Toronto Centred Region. The problem is that noise from aircraft flight-operations is felt to be objectionable in the adjacent-communities. It is also questionable if Malton is equipped or can be made to accommodate the unforeseen possible developments in aviation technology to the year 2000.[8]

He did not specify the "unforeseen possible developments". A new airport and its supporting infrastructure is therefore a very costly venture. If the airport is viewed as an isolated venture and if the federal government must finance it by itself, it would be more difficult to achieve adequate revenues from the aviation service to offset these capital costs and thereby to meet the financial objectives of making air service self-sustaining. If, however, the airport is viewed as part of a much larger regional development such as the Toronto Centred Region, the combined uses and benefits should prove financially advantageous.

Further, Beinhacker reiterated an earlier recommendation that the government of Canada acquire the airport and that the province protect the noiseland. He felt that the adjoining urban community would grow with the airport. He proposed a "Design for Aviation". "The concept was to acquire land for a major airport facility, to develop an intercontinental airport for charter and some scheduled activity now and to preserve flexibility of expanding the role of the new airport if necessary in the future." He used many sites around Metro as illustrative examples.

As each of the four prime sites selected previously presented peculiar difficulties, the federal Minister of Transport directed that a document be prepared to describe the alternatives, and that a final choice be left in abeyance. The provincial government on the other hand reviewed the issue under the caption "Summary Report on Status of Airport Planning" and outlined the following options:

- Expand Malton only.
- Build a major facility at one of the external sites and continue Malton in a short-term role.
- Expand Malton and purchase a land bank at one of the external sites. This land would be for the purpose of ensuring environmental control, i.e., if the developing aircraft tech-

nology does not succeed in containing noise and air pollution, then Malton's role would be curtailed and the alternative expanded.

• Expand Malton and develop a system of regional airports with Malton having a central and long-term role. Primary regional airports would be located at Oshawa and Hamilton.

• Close Malton and develop a new facility at one external site (post 1982).

The report recommended that in the Ontario government's evaluation a preferred solution lies in a combination of these options—alternative 2 using site B with option 4.

This would involve a moderate expansion of Malton beyond the current phase II, together with the development of an eastern airport site as soon as possible to serve as a regional airport.*

This alternative will cost less, because the new facility will be smaller. Nevertheless, an eastern stimulus required by the regional concept would be obtained. Any later plan for a regional airport in the west could be tied to further studies of airport requirements in southwestern Ontario."[9]

The approval of this decision meant that there was going to be not just one airport but "a system of airports". The task force then recommended two new sites. Beverley Township in the southwestern section of the region and Pickering township in the northeast. The southwest site appeared to be particularly appealing. In a letter to J.A. Howard of Toronto Airports Project Office, June 30, 1971, George Sladek, one of the members of the task force, observed:

In the case of the Pickering site, a two runway airport appears to pose little difficulty. A four runway airport also appears possible but with considerably greater difficulty . . . . I believe that Pickering site is more likely to interfere with community development plans than Beverley site and therefore some effort should be spent on former site to understand the long range plan for this region and to determine the impact of the airport on these plans.

In the appraisal of the Pickering-township site-evaluation, the following sections speak for themselves.

*Regional was not defined.

With the exception of the community of Brougham, the entire area is devoted to agriculture and is under cultivation. The farms are of high quality and farm buildings are generally of good quality and well maintained. There is considerable residential development in the form of good quality homes, some on large plots, built along the secondary road systems. Most of the secondary roads are improved gravel surface, but considerable mileage is hard surfaced and all appear to be well travelled. . . .

There could be considerable opposition to airport development at this location from gentlemen and other farmers because of very considerable effort and money invested on farm improvements.

Apropos local impact of the airport, no special problems were anticipated. "The farms are of high quality and there is very considerable high class rural residential development. For these reasons acquisition may be difficult and costly but the arguments are more likely to be of an economic rather than of a sociological nature." Finally, "the development area . . . is probably too restricted for a four-runway airport with 5,000 foot preparations."

A Progress Report (August 20, 1971)[10] makes interesting reading. It pointed out that the "air space in the vicinity of the Northeast site is considerably more congested, and this coupled with a fairly narrow separation (30 air miles) is expected to constrain operations". The northeast site proved to be more restrictive from the viewpoints of noise coverage, land use, and topography. "While the site is quite generous for a two-runway airport, it becomes difficult to cater for four runways, and there is insufficient area for six runways."

As for the Beverley Township areas, there are no major topographical constraints at this site — drainage is generally to the south, but because of the Conservation Area it may be necessary to develop the site drainage so as not to affect the swamp. Furthermore land acquisitions for the two sites vary. In Beverley township, 25,800 acres were valued at $40,960,000, whereas at Pickering 19,400 acres were worth $55,500,000 at the same time.[11] The land in the northwest was obtainable in larger quantities and at a cheaper rate.

The choice of both the Beverley and Pickering sites were developments from the new criteria. It was desirable to pick sites that fitted into regional transportation systems and were located close to the major market. But more important they would offer more than the original four and get less costly. In October 1971, a provincial report "Review of the Proposed Sites E and F — Regional Development Plan" evaluated the two sites according to the Toronto Centred Region plan. As far as Pickering airport site is concerned, it partly satisfies the requirement for "general economic stimulus in the eastern corridor but falls short to an extent which may have the effect of stimulating growth in and adjacent to Metropolitan Toronto, rather than in and near Oshawa, as desired."[12]

The goal here was to stimulate Oshawa and subsequent growth in Ajax, Audley, and Cedarwood. The report also warned that partly because of "the power of an airport to focus growth", selection of the Beverley site would "detract from the effectiveness of government measures to stimulate growth and services east of Toronto" and might cause growing pains in the adjacent cities. Hence it was suggested that if the western airport could not be prevented, it should at least be delayed so that the east may gain the momentum.

The decision to go ahead with the eastern site was made in spite of the fact that the December 1971 report on the three-airport system saw the consultants recommending the southwest approach over Pickering. It also said that if there was to be only one site — southwest was the preferred site. A comparison with the northeast showed that Pickering was not as suitable as the Beverley site.

With all the evidence before them on December 21, 1971, the Honourable Donald Jamieson and the Honourable Charles MacNaughton met and determined a course of action. They agreed that a new major airport would be located at the north Pickering site! Malton would remain a major international airport! Consideration was to be given to various proposals to upgrade air services to southwestern Ontario!

The final decision to proceed with an international airport at Pickering would not seem to have had a feasibility study. The site would not support an international operation of dimensions necessary to return revenue justifying capital expense. The process to the eastern border of Metro denied the basic thrust of the *Design for Development* which saw a stimulus much farther to the east. The hurried environmental and social-impact studies ignored or missed the magnitude of the social disruption that would result — and caused a stream of protests which would be heard from sea to sea.

Environmentally it was believed in official circles that Pickering was less attractive on only one count — the soil is better than that of Beverley. However, no sound environmental survey had been done, much less a study of the impact on the community. Speaking before the Standing Committee on Supply, April 17th, in the Ontario House, the Honourable J.A.C. Auld could not cite any environmental studies that had been done aside from the Ontario Water Resources Control survey. However, position papers prepared by POP showed the disastrous effect that siting the airport in this area would have on conservation areas and on wildlife and recreational facilities for the Ontario public in the Pickering region.

Resultant from intense discussions between the province of Ontario and the Government of Canada it was agreed that a system of airports should be developed. In addition to building a new one at Pickering, the airports at London, Hamilton, and Windsor would be expanded. This led subsequently to the "annex of understanding" between the federal Minister of Transport and the Treasurer and Minister of Economics and Intergovernmental Affairs of Ontario, and the public announcement on March 2, 1972. The main points of this agreement are as follows:

March 1, 1972

ANNEX OF UNDERSTANDING

1. The Governments of Canada and Ontario have agreed to the establishment of a major airport in Pickering Township in an area roughly between a line just north of Highway 7 in the south, north to the Uxbridge/Pickering Township boundary and between the Little Rouge Creek on the west and East Duffin Creek on the east. Each of our governments is committed to carrying out certain actions in respect to this development. The extent of commitment of funds in any one year is subject to the necessary parliamentary and legislative authorities being received by the respective governments.

2. The Federal Government will acquire through the Federal Expropriation Act an area of some 18,000 acres. Under this Act, the Federal Government will register Notice of Intention to

expropriate this land. The exact area to be acquired for airport operations will include all land within the 115 CNR (Composite Noise Rating) contour.

3. The Government of Ontario has agreed to act, within the full extent of its legislative authority, to ensure that lands exposed to 95 CNR contour or equivalent and above will be controlled to prevent development inconsistent with airport operations. The Government of Ontario has agreed to issue a Ministerial Order under Section 32 of the Planning Act, subject to item 4 below, establishing development controls on lands to which the statute is applicable within the area between the CNR contour of 95 or its equivalent for the final runway configuration for ultimate airport development and the airport boundary. It will also recommend against local zoning changes or severances inconsistent with such development controls and will not approve any official plans, or plans of subdivisions inconsistent with such development controls. The Government of Ontario will discuss with local municipalities the development or modification of official plans so as to seek to make them consistent with airport operations. When such consistency is achieved, the Minister may withdraw direct provincial controls.

4. For land between the 95 CNR contour or equivalent, and the airport boundary, the Federal Government has agreed to assume financial responsibility for claims that may result from existing developed and operative uses being incompatible with the uses permitted under the development controls introduced under section 3 above.

5. The Government of Ontario has agreed to provide basic services normally provided by the Province to the airport boundaries, subject to any federal-provincial sharing agreements now in force or which may be developed.

6. The Federal Government accepts the principle of its responsibility for meeting certain incremental costs uniquely attributable to services and facilities required by the airport but outside the airport boundary, as mutually agreed.

7. The Federal Government has agreed to assume financial responsibility for the relocation of certain services from the airport lands. The exact sums involved will be determined when the nature of the services dislocated has been established, and the extent to which such services could continue to be used despite passing through airport property has been determined.

8. The Federal Government has agreed that there will be a joint federal-provincial study of all transportation requirements to serve the airport and its related communities and an agreement will later be reached on an appropriate sharing of expenditures

on transportation facilities. The Federal Government has recognized a particular interest in the provision of rapid transit facilities.

9. The Government of Ontario has agreed to acquire some 25,000 acres of land adjacent to the airport for the development of a new community proposed by the Toronto Centred Region Plan, as modified to incorporate the new northeast airport, and for transportation and service corridors associated with that plan.

10. Through relevant federal statutes and programs, now in force or to be developed, the Federal Government has agreed to contribute financially to the cost of land assembled by the Government of Ontario for the purposes stated in 9 above.

11. The Governments of Canada and Ontario have agreed to a joint study of potential use of the Island Airport.

12. The Governments of Canada and Ontario have agreed that the existing Federal-Provincial Committee should be continued to study cooperative aspects of implementation.

Why was this site chosen?

Here is the Ontario government's answer released March 2, 1972 — the day of the simultaneous announcement in Ottawa and Queen's Park.

The selection of any airport site in Canada rests primarily with the Federal Ministry of Transport and is based on flying characteristics, safety considerations and convenience to the area to be served. At the same time, the Ontario Government wanted a location to fit well with its plan for the Toronto Centred Region. Numerous alternatives were considered, and the Pickering Township site was chosen because:

• It is an excellent site, consistent with safety and other aeronautical considerations.
• Of all the proposed sites, it is closest to Toronto, and therefore provides the easiest accessibility.
• It is close enough to Lake Ontario and to several transportation routes so as to keep service costs (water, sewerage, roads) at reasonable levels — lower, in fact, than they would be at any other sites considered.
• No major communities will be seriously affected by expropriation or by noise from the airport.

What impact will the new airport have on towns such as Markham, Stouffville, Richmond Hill, Ajax and Oshawa?

Adjustments to runway alignments will protect both Markham and Stouffville from aircraft noise levels that might bother existing communities. Residents of more distant towns, such as Richmond Hill — will be conscious of planes overhead, but no more so than the people of, say, Toronto are when planes are over the city. Nor will Ajax, Oshawa, or other communities to the south experience any noticeable noise. On the other hand, a few villages right at the site, such as Brougham, will be included in the land purchased for the airport.

Except for those villages in and around the site, communities in the general vicinity will enjoy an acceleration of the development they hoped for and expected in the immediate years ahead.

What about the people who own land in the area?

Apart from the federal government's purchase of the land for the airport itself, the provincial government considers it essential to buy up all the lands needed to create an efficient, attractive, and fully integrated community in the area. To prevent costly inflation of land prices in the area, the government intends to acquire all the land which, in the long run, will benefit both the new community itself and the people of Ontario, as a whole.

To what extent is the province committed to providing highways and other services?

The Ontario government intends to build Highway 407 as an east-west route, several miles north of the Macdonald-Cartier Freeway (401) and parallel to it. Highway 407 will serve the entire urbanized, eastern part of the Toronto Centred Region. The province also intends to build another freeway running northeast from Toronto. This highway may be started earlier than originally intended, because of the decision to locate the airport in the northeast.

NEW TORONTO AIRPORT in the
TORONTO CENTRED
REGION PLAN

Government of Ontario
Department of Treasury & Economics

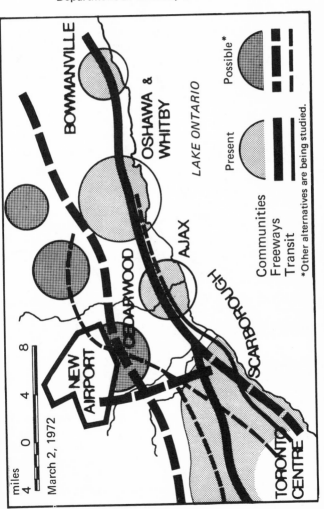

KEY LANDS and TRANSPORTATION
NEW TORONTO AIRPORT

Government of Ontario
Department of Treasury & Economics

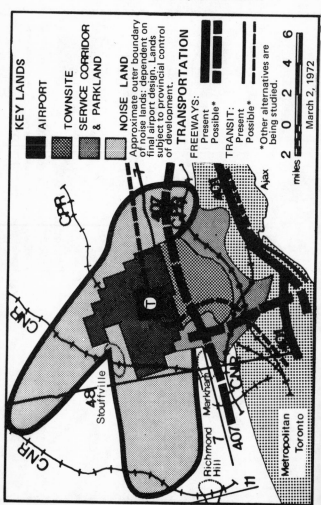

KEY LANDS

AIRPORT
TOWNSITE
SERVICE CORRIDOR & PARKLAND
NOISE LAND

Approximate outer boundary of noise lands: dependent on final airport design. Lands subject to provincial control of development.

TRANSPORTATION

FREEWAYS:
Present
Possible*

TRANSIT:
Present
Possible*

*Other alternatives are being studied.

miles 2 0 2 4 6

March 2, 1972

CPR

CNR

CNR

CNR

Ajax

Stouffville
48

Markham
407
7

Richmond Hill
11

Metropolitan Toronto

New rapid-transit lines to serve new urban centres in the area northeast of the city will be constructed. One of these lines would run through Cedarwood, serving the airport and extending to other towns further east.

Meanwhile, the province would make sure that Cedarwood and other surrounding communities are bounded by parklands and other open spaces, not only to provide residents with some pleasant countryside nearby, but to provide land for transportation and other services.

How much will the whole development cost?

Only the federal government can reveal the likely cost of the airport itself. As for surrounding developments, the Ontario government has not yet arrived at complete estimates. Land acquisitions costs are likely to amount to about $70 million. Developments of the new community and services (water, sewerage, access roads) will cost several hundred million additional dollars. These costs are not to be burdens for taxpayers, however; much of the development will be financed by private capital.

Will Cedarwood be developed by the government?

This has yet to be decided. Probably, the province will decide to work in partnership with private developers. Whatever course is chosen, the province will play a significant role.

4. The Gathering Protest

Bob Almack, Queen's '74, hurried to the bus station through the slush and ice. It would take him about four hours to get to Pickering and then he would have to get a ride up the Brock Road to his father's house. It was important that he get there tonight before 8 p.m.

He was looking forward to going out on the fields tomorrow to see if the snow cover had lasted. The wheat he had sown in the fifty-acre field would provide him with his fees for next year.

That was the one good thing about grain farming as opposed to cattle raising. After you had done your work in the fall you could leave the farm and go to school and do the thrashing during the summer holidays. Old Tom Carter came around with his swather about the last week of August and pretty soon there were 2,000 bushels of York Star on the way to the Claremont Co-op. Last year the price had been pretty good because the moisture content had been below 14 per cent, and that was because they had got the grain off quickly. What with a good snow cover and early rains this spring he hoped to do even better. After all, fees were going up in the fall anyway.

But more important than that was this radio broadcast he had heard in part which said something about an airport in Pickering. That would be a total disaster. Airplanes can't live with birds and any farmer knows that plowing

*and reaping brings birds. So if you are going to have an
airport you will have to kill the birds (like they do with
the owls at Malton) or change farming practices.*

*The wheat he grew was grown on land which he had
worked up carefully over the past six years. It was good
land because he had spent money and time on cultivating,
enriching, and keeping it clean.*

*He reached home just in time to go down the road with
his father to the meeting at Melody Farm.*

On Thursday, March 2, the federal and provincial governments announced the site of the proposed new airport, and
for a few hours the shock waves that hit Pickering rever-
berated throughout Ontario and parts of Canada. Welcomed
by some, the airport was anathema to others, whose rage and
anger soon resolved into organized resistance.

After a day of telephone calls the first meeting took place
on Friday evening at Melody Farm, a beautiful 125-year-old
home near Claremont, where, according to local historians, a
bell was rung to announce the rebellion of 1837. Eighty
people passed a resolution to oppose any airport in southern
Ontario, formed the committees that were to become People
or Planes, and set a public meeting for the following Tuesday,
March 7, in Brougham, a town that would simply vanish
beneath a concrete tidal wave of progress.

On Saturday afternoon the Steering Committee met to
plan the meeting. Radio technicians provided two-way
speakers connecting from the United Church to the Town
Hall in case of an overflow crowd. Guest speakers were
contacted. A CBC producer provided an amplifier and jet
engine soundtrack. The news media were contacted. Five
hundred copies of an article by Anthony Jay, concerning the
airport struggle at Cublington, England, were printed.
Monday night 300 citizens attended the Pickering Municipal
Council meeting to encourage passage of a unanimous resolution stating "that this Council is opposed to the construction
of a second Toronto airport in the location suggested".

On Tuesday at 8 p.m., one thousand citizens arrived in Brougham. Both halls were packed. "People or Planes" was the theme. Mr. Norman Cafik, Liberal M.P. for Ontario Country, stated his unalterable opposition to the airport. He did not want to see the rape of this countryside. He promised to press for full disclosure of all technical information but suggested it was really a provincial decision. Mr. Bill Newman, the Conservative member in the Ontario legislature, affirmed his complete opposition to the plan and assured the meeting that he would request full disclosure of the feasibility studies. Mr. Newman suggested that the federal government had the final say. The Chairman, Dr. Charles Godfrey, commented that the members seemed to be playing the Indian shell game with responsibility.

Godfrey warned the audience that this would be a long, hard fight. Hugh J. Miller pointed out that "the government was replacing something priceless (the top six inches of soil) with something expensive". Bill Lishman, an artist, called for citizens' action to "keep the stench of the city out of Brougham's nostrils". A group including the Reeve, several councillors, and even the federal candidate, Frank McGee, stood up and drew cheers when it affirmed that the secrecy of the decision and the lack of consultation was a reprehensible act.

A brush-fire enthusiasm swept through the riding during the following days. Local branches were formed in the threatened communities; seven lawyers, one of them a judge, volunteered for the legal committee. Forty artists began preparing poster designs and publicity, and a host of citizens offered to serve in any capacity. Public meetings of a thousand or more people became a weekly appearance. POP quickly joined other meetings to plague speakers with the airport question. A routine appearance by the Prime Minister at a riding talk in Scarborough on March 28th was turned into an airport grilling by a group of Poppers. The Prime Minister promised that the federal government would not go ahead with the airport if the majority of people in the Toronto area were opposed. He agreed that Toronto was just "keeping up with the Jones's". Montreal had a new airport. The Torontonians wanted one, too.

At the same time the Ontario government was distributing a tabloid in the Pickering area assuring its residents that the decision was final.

If nothing else, one thing was clear: almost everyone concerned was confused, uncertain, and badly informed. But POP could only scream objections. With calculated skill it played on fears of aircraft crashing into the Atomic Energy Plant at Pickering; adversely affecting the new zoo; turning a peaceful countryside into a noisy concrete jungle. This tactic was necessary because they had no other weapons. The federal and provincial governments stubbornly refused to give out details of why or how the decision was reached.

POP's primary objective at this time was to educate themselves and the public and to ask and get answers to certain crucial questions: was a second airport really needed? why Pickering? why was there no public and local government participation in the decisions? On March 27th, telegrams were sent to Prime Minister Trudeau and Premier Davis asking that expropriations be stopped until studies of the situation had been made.

POP had by now become a permanent organization with Dr. Charles M. Godfrey as Chairman. The organization was based on geographical "cells" — one to each area affected — either inside the airport area or the airport city (Cedarwood) or the noise areas. In addition, each special interest group — the artists, the "creative", the legal group — had a representative. Each of the cells sent a representative to the Steering Committee which was the Parliament of POP. A secretariat was formed. A treasurer and auditor were appointed; several key committee chairmen — legal, publicity, youth, technical, diplomatic, senior citizens, environmental, creative, and fund raising — came together as an Executive Committee. The fund raising was given priority because it was realized that to make two governments change their minds would take a lot of persuasion, a lot of pressure, a lot of public participation, a lot of legal finesse. A budget of $90,000 was struck.

J.J. Robinette, the lawyer associated with the Stop Spadina Movement, was retained as counsel. On April 4th at a Toronto City Hall meeting with CORRA (Confederation of Residents and Ratepayers Association) it was resolved that the two groups had much in common and that collaboration was possible.

Signs and posters began to proliferate and a letter-writing campaign was directed at Trudeau and the main *villians* of the piece, federal Transport Minister Don Jamieson and provincial Treasurer Darcy McKeough. Writing to Trudeau on April 13th, Peter A. Jones reflected POP's position when he said, in part: "Now that the public are demanding and receiving more specific technical data on the need and location of such a second air transport facility, it is becoming increasingly clear that this is a political decision rather than an economically feasible scheme) . . . To confiscate prime farmland, to displace by noise pollution the tremendous number of people not expropriated (not to mention those to be expropriated for highways) to disrupt the balance of nature so that animals would not be able to reproduce due to the high noise levels, to destroy three conservation areas and seriously affect eight others, and to jeopardize the new $26,000,000 zoo all for the sake of political considerations is indeed criminal." Jones also insisted that the only logical solution was the government's original plan, inexplicably vetoed by the Ontario government, to expand Malton's facilities.

As pieces of information were pieced together by the POP Technical Committee, an overall strategy began to take shape. A "leaked" report helped to confirm the suspicion that the Pickering airport was not necessary, because Malton had sufficient potential to see the air traveller through to A.D. 2000. This was perhaps the fundamental premise of POP's campaign, which was gaining momentum with innumerable letters to the editor, press releases, television and radio appearances, town meetings, fund-raising activities, and interviews with government officials. Still there was a lack of basic information. The supply of surreptitious phone calls, documents appearing mysteriously at POP headquarters or words spoken in confidence was not enough to mount a good case. In a series of public appeals and telegrams the Minister of Transport was asked to give out information to POP. He finally agreed (although the provincial Secretary said he would not release any reports), and arrangements for a meeting between the Minister and

POP were made by Barney Danson and Norm Cafik.

The meeting was preceded by an all-night session by POP members in a room in an adjoining hotel which looked onto the Ministry's offices. A great deal of activity went on in both areas.

Both parties, the Minister of Transport and the Chairman of POP were very much aware of the niceties of politics during the meeting. They sat at each end of a table — thirty feet apart — and conducted their discussion so that all members could hear. The Minister's party consisted of all of the senior officials of the department and Mr. Beinhacker, the consultant from Kates Peat Marwick & Co.

In the opening minutes the Minister pointed out that the decision to site the airport at Pickering was the best advice his department could come up with — an unhappy compromise — which had to be taken in view of the expected great increase of air traffic by the year 2000. He sympathized with the members of POP and others in the area who would be affected, but pointed out that his department had to make plans for the welfare of a large number of citizens in the future.

POP had prepared a series of questions which were put to the Minister. It was emphasized that this was a fact-finding mission only because there had been such a paucity of information passed out. In effect, the questions asked for all the supporting documents that had been used by the government in arriving at the decision. Mr. Jamieson agreed that these be made available. However, he pointed out that requests would have to be made specifically for each document as he had "four rooms full" of documents. One thing emerged from the meeting quite strongly. Mr. Beinhacker was the major source of information and most likely of decision-making in the whole process. On many occasions it was necessary to turn to him for an answer.

The meeting lasted four hours and fifteen minutes, which, in view of the fact that this was caucus day, was undoubtedly an attempt by the Minister to answer all questions as fairly as possible. POP ended by requesting whether there had been an unfeasibility study performed on the decision. The government was taken aback at this suggestion and pointed out that

49

there had been no formal unfeasibility study but this was built into any decision-making process. POP then offered to conduct an unfeasibility study and suggested inasmuch as funds had been made available for a feasibility study it seemed only fair that the government should do the same for another study which would help reach a wise decision. Mr. Jamieson refused the money request but did agree to provide any information or resource personnel that POP could use.

By the time the POP delegation had emerged on the street a press release from the government had announced further details of the decision, and the documents for which POP had come to Ottawa had been made available to the country as a whole.

The unfeasibility study was a prime concern of POP's technical committee, which produced in the following weeks a number of well researched briefs on "Growth", "The Need for Another Airport", "Alternate Transportation: STOL and Rail", "Site Selection", "Ecology and the Pickering Airport", "Farming", and "The Pickering Airport and the Toronto Centred Regional Plan", which together constituted POP's Unfeasibility Study.

These documents and many other studies fell on deaf government ears. Repeated statements from the offices of McKeough and Jamieson pointed out that the decision was inviolate and could not be reversed. Representations from societies such as the Federation of Ontario Naturalists, ratepayers groups throughout Toronto, Pollution Probe, the Toronto Citizens Forum and CORRA, received no acknowledgments. Statements by members of the Canadian Airline Pilots Association and the International Air Transport Association had no effect.

The original strategy of POP had been to arouse the populace to object to the airport on the basis that it was not needed and was not wanted. In addition the Airport City — Cedarwood — was denied. The tactic to bring this opinion home to the government was to write to Prime Minister Trudeau and to federal and provincial elected representatives. It was felt by some of the strategy board that the decision to site the airport had been made in a hurry and that the government really did not have sufficient factual material to back up the decision. (Indeed the material handed out at Ottawa had all been dated that day.) Accordingly, it was reasoned that possibly Jamieson had been on an ego trip and had not fully consulted all members of the Cabinet. The statement of Trudeau in Scarborough, cited earlier, tended to reinforce this opinion.

Thus there was a tactic to involve the public in a massive protest by mail. At the same time it was reasoned that many members of the government were amenable to reason. A series of meetings were set up by the Diplomatic Committee with members and candidates. The imminence of a federal election gave these meetings a higher charge than the normal state.

The third approach was via the legal arm. By the terms of the Expropriation Act of Canada, a Hearing Officer had to be appointed to register objections by all concerned (anybody in Canada) by the decision. The Legal Committee, acting on the advice of Mr. Robinette, drew up an objection form and began plans for a canvas of a large area in order to have in Mr. Robinette's hand a substantial number of objections when the Hearing was to be held. However, Mr. Robinette pointed out that, as the law was written, the Expropriation Act did not provide an opportunity for an inquiry. Rather, all that could be done was to register objections. He pointed out that he could not have a good run at the problem with such strictures.

Acting from this advice, Mr. Robinette was asked to request the Minister for a Public Inquiry under the Public Inquiries Act. Such a tactic would insure an objective hearing by an impartial judge using normal rules of evidence. In addition, witnesses required by POP or the government would be paid by the government. This request was put in a letter to Jamieson.

It became obvious that the interim strategy of POP was to demand a Public Inquiry in order that all the facts could be put before the public. The request was refused by Jamieson (and also by Trudeau) on the basis that it would represent an abdication of government to a non-elected tribunal. POP pointed out that under the terms of a Public Inquiry the findings were not binding on the government but could be used as an input of information. Jamieson remained obdurate.

Milton Mowbray, a member of the legal committee said: "What discourages me is the sort of pig-headed approach some of these government officials are taking. They're putting themselves in a position where it will be very difficult for them to back down gracefully." And for this reason, Mowbray continued, POP's tactics would just have to be agitation for the next while.

Agitation was indeed the order of the early summer months. A Spring Festival in May brought thousands of people to the Township to tour old homes and get a taste of country life. Press releases poured out of POP headquarters in Claremont, especially in response to government pamphlets like that of May 24th which offered two years rent-free accommodation to affected home owners if they sold before expropriation. On May 18th a 100-foot Ministry of Transport survey tower, located three miles west of Brougham, was pulled down, though this action is not necessarily blamed on POP. A walk-a-thon in the area around Green River was conducted on June 3rd, and on June 15th traffic on University Avenue stood still as a mock funeral procession, carrying coffins, went to Queen's Park. On the coffins were the names of the towns *murdered* by the airport.

Similar events on June 22nd and July 5th culminated in a monster rally in City Hall Square, complete with clowns representing Jamieson and McKeough, bands, speeches, and on one occasion a donkey labelled Jamieson. Thirty non-POP speakers representing ratepayers groups were on the platform.

A car outfitted with an amplifier drove through the streets of Stouffville broadcasting the sound of jet engines. When threatened with arrest the driver, Margaret Godfrey, said, "Arrest Air Canada too. It makes more noise." Ten thousand "information bits" were mailed to area residents and a house-to-house canvass was conducted to document objections to expropriation and to raise funds. A war of signs, posters, and buttons appeared on township trees, walls, and breasts as the various POP slogans — "Airport No", "We Will Not Be Moved", "Ontario: A Place to Stand or a Place to

Land" — were opposed by those of a group called **POW** (Progress Over Welfare), which was angrily for the airport and against POP. POW, which grew out of the many struggling farmers who were happy to be expropriated, claimed that POP stood for Poverty Over Prosperity. According to POP, POW meant Pave Our World.

While providing comic relief and a cartoon-like delineation of issues, all of this brouhaha had a serious objective: to bring to the attention of the public a possibly catastrophic decision pertaining not just to Pickering but to Toronto and Canada, a decision which Mr. Stephen Lewis characterized in the Ontario Legislature on June 26th as "A piece of economic expansion which is one of the most destructive pieces of economic planning, one of the greatest errors in judgement, which this government has entered into."

Behind the rallies and concerts, the fund-raising antics, and publicity gimmicks, the serious business of POP was always going on. Experts and resource people were being enrolled. All available information was being acquired — government and private technical and environmental studies, here and abroad, relating to airports and airport expansion, along with government speeches and opinions from all interested and disinterested individuals and groups. A London *Sunday Times* primer on how to fight bureaucracy and block an airport was reprinted and distributed.

Taking a leaf from the government, three newspaper supplements were published by POP, which lampooned, berated, cajoled, and attacked the decision for fifty thousand readers. Letters by the thousands were sent and received to and from professionals, scientists, and politicians. Letters were sent to virtually every newspaper in Canada, either explaining the POP position or responding, sometimes angrily, to uninformed editorials (like that of *The Toronto Sun* on April 5th) which oscillated between stupidity and ignorance with such statements as: "Basically, most people agree that a new airport will be needed" and "Most of the citizens affected seem satisfied they've been fairly treated by the government."

Even worse than this, however, was such government doubletalk as that of Darcy McKeough, in a speech to the

Legislature on June 6th when he somehow reasoned that the new airport "far from representing a departure from our original strategy . . . . is a step in the implementation of the Toronto Centred Regional Plan".

The odds against POP and other opponents of the airport and its complementary city of 200,000 people were directly proportionate to McKeough's ability to deny that the decision is a violation of the Toronto Centred Plan which he had previously supported: ". . . our policy is to maintain land use essentially in its present form, that is mainly agricultural, recreational and open space" (*Status Report,* August 1971). How was POP to communicate with a ministry so much out of touch with the crucial issues that it could issue a statement assuring the people in all seriousness that the jets would not hurt the new zoo.

This reluctance of the government to put all the facts on the table heightened suspicions of the POP group. Why was there a need to conceal facts? Why was there a need to be less than frank in the vital matters of expropriation hearing? By the terms of the Expropriation Act the hearing officer could be appointed to register objections of land owners. Nowhere did it say that there would be a process or inquiry that would indicate a need by the federal government for the property. Unless some special action in the terms of the Expropriation Act were made or some special consideration was to be given to POP objectors, the hearing under the Expropriation Act would amount to no more than a routine filing of objections. Yet the government kept insisting there would be opportunity for a full hearing and on this basis denied a public inquiry. At no time was an undertaking given from the government to POP or other groups of objectors that there would be an opportunity to question the need for an airport. Similarly, at no time would there be an opportunity for the government to show clear need of the Pickering Site as opposed to other sites.

POP's clamour for a public inquiry was finally met by the announcement of a "public hearing". However, this announcement was confused. At no time did the Minister of Transport state in the House or outside the House that the "hearing" would be a hearing of necessity along the lines of a public inquiry. POP insisted that there was a necessity for a public inquiry and that the government's offer would not lead to a clear definition of needs.

It would be tempting to say that most of the problem was one of communication — that POP felt it could not trust the Ministry of Transport because it had not been frank in its dealings. Similarly, the Ministry of Transport could not put all its cards on the table because POP and other groups might pick on certain areas and distort them out of proportion in an election year.

These positions were rapidly leading to a polarization of opinions five months after the announcement of the airport so that no matter what evidence was brought up by either of the contestants, there could be a solution only by an objective independent body.

There was a tone of regret in the POP announcements during the early election days. In part this tone was generated by disappointment in the processes of government. A disappointment that was heightened by the realization that somewhere along the line, the philosophy of W.H. Huck, Administrator, Canadian Air Transportation, had been changed.

We have to be "people-oriented" in our planning.

Because of this the Canadian Air Transportation Administration is taking care that in every new airport construction project in which the Ministry of Transport is involved such as Ste. Scholastique, Quebec, the planned new Calgary terminal and the new major airport system being considered for the Toronto area, the views of the people who live on and near the possible sites are taken into account. Citizens' groups, municipal and provincial governments are all included in the preliminary consultations on these undertakings.

While such consultation may introduce delays, we feel that it is absolutely necessary. From the standpoint of the property owner who may face expropriation, or the neighbour who doesn't want 400-passenger airliners thundering over his home on takeoff or landing, an airport is something he doesn't need. Everyone wants it located in somebody else's neighbourhood. [*Journal of Canadian Aeronautics and Space Institute,* October 1971.]

5. The Politics of Expediency

The telephone had been ringing steadily for the past two hours. Anne Wanstall turned it over to Aileen to give her ear a rest. The terrible news of the proposed airport had been broadcast and already the word had spread to the farthest corners of the township.

Aileen Adams and Anne had lived in this house, Melody Farm, for eight years. When they bought it a group of friends had helped them clean it up, scrape off the paint, and rebuild the windows. It was an old house. It was built in 1867 by the Barclay Family.

George Barclay, an ordained Baptist minister, had come to the Brock Road in 1817. The family settled on the back half of Elizabeth Matthews' grant. First they built a log cabin and then with an enlarging family built Ever Green Villa which was renamed Melody Farm many years later.

The house was built when fireplaces were going out of style and stoves were used for heating. But Eli, his son, had put a fireplace in the kitchen because the family spent most of their time there. It was alight this afternoon as Anne and Aileen spread the word of the meeting to be held that night.

The old timbered floors would groan under the weight of eighty people crammed into the small house. The chimney, beside which Aunt Line had kept the cathartics for the children, would blister from the wood in the grate and the indignation of the crowd.

Our political process is not a hodge-podge of political experience or the institutionalization of disaster. It is an accumulation of historical experience, an expression of pragmatic principles, and the embodiment of a long process of trial and error. If the system works well, society is the gainer; if it fails, society is the loser. Because the political system is as complex as the social system, it is sometimes subject to clever manipulation and may prove unresponsive to obvious need. Because government may become arbitrary, unenlightened, and even out of touch, democracy must serve as a leavener. "Men live in society in order that each individual can realize himself to the maximum."

The ideal of democracy is that power should flow from discussion and that it should be a means of realizing the common good. Even in a society of angels there might be disagreement about the constitution of the common good, but as Prime Minister Trudeau wrote: "What holds us to democracy is not that it is faultless but that it is less faulty than any other system." To be precise, "democracy is the only form of government that fully respects the dignity of man. . . . It alone is based on the belief that all men can be made fit to participate, directly or indirectly, in the guidance of the society of which they are members." Our political system is durable and we seem to like it. With all its weaknesses, "it does nonetheless provide a high probability that any active and legitimate group will make itself heard at some stage in the process of decision."

From the point of view of the people of Pickering Township, Canadian democracy has been set back by the secret manoeuverings that preceeded the announcement of Airport II. Vital information has been withheld from the public; the residents of the area have not been consulted; and there has been an absence of the painstaking research that characterized other regions, especially regarding the ecological and sociological. As early as 1967, and in the two months prior to the announcement of March 2nd, real-estate records indicate a phenomenal rise in buying and selling outside the expropriation area. Democracy demands that governments be made accountable; concern dictates that Canadians be made aware of all the factors; integrity dictates

57

that the birthright of the people of Pickering Township mus not be sold for a mess of pottage.

Given the cloak of secrecy that has been pulled over some of the negotiation sessions, the complex factors that entered into the many points of view, the styles and philosophies o the chief policy-makers, and the very nature of our federal system — the shared jurisdiction and shifts in the pendulum of power from the federal to provincial governments or vice versa — it is not always easy to reconstruct the events that lead to Pickering. As a result of complex interviews, tele phone conversations, tips and rap sessions, the following collage emerges:

1. The Federal Position

Mindful of provincial as well as community reaction to the Ste Scholastique Airport, the federal government was eager by late 1971 to avoid a confrontation with the new premier and government of Ontario. Rising unemployment, tough anti-inflation measures, and a general impression of sluggishness had reduced the Trudeau government's effectiveness and popularity. On the other hand, Davis's government was riding on a crest of popular support — it had stopped the Spadina expressway; it won a resounding victory at the polls; and in speeches and debates it hinted at taking a tough new stand towards Ottawa.

Federal negotiations were handled by Mr. Donald Jamieson and his Ministry of Transport. As the sole Liberal M.P. from Newfoundland and administrator of a large and often controversial department, Mr. Jamieson has come under a great deal of pressure. For one, a number of Toronto Liberal M.P.s quietly demanded that just as Montreal merited a second airport so did Toronto. The federal Minister was particularly anxious to do something in the Toronto area, but was hard put as to just what should be done and where. He was particularly incensed by charges that Montreal was getting too much while Toronto was being increasingly by-passed. Many of his own officials were uneasy about the technical requirement for a new airport in the Toronto region this was part of the reason why the Ministry of Transport was reluctant to make public a number of airport studies), but the hard-pressed Minister was willing to effect any meaningful compromise. Transportation is a crucial problem for an increasingly urban society, and yet the Ministry of Transport is not the most dynamic portfolio. The relationship between it and the Canadian Transport Commission is sometimes blurred, and it is not unusual for the two groups to be at loggerheads. The C.T.C., a regulatory commission, has been given the responsibility for a great deal of research, yet some of this research is duplicated in the Ministry of Transport.

A crucial problem for the Ministry is its failure to undertake long-range planning. It is one thing to plan airports but it is another to work out an industrial strategy, so that our urban communities are not disturbed by noise or overrun by machines. The Ministry of Transport should be actively engaged in long-term studies on urban transportation, aircraft technology, and the various technical options. What is being done at the moment is too piecemeal; what is required is a broader and more integrated approach.

Many of the Ministry of Transport difficulties stem from the fact that the senior levels need to be strengthened and more authority delegated. This would reduce its reliance on outside consultants, especially those with an axe to grind coming from large firms. The firm of Kates Peat Marwick & Co. played a crucial role in the Ste. Scholastique and Pickering choices. This firm, listed as management consultants, have built airports in Greece, Brazil, and Ste. Scholastique in Montreal. At the latter, they did location and capacity design and contracted out the rest. In fact, one of the leading members of the company, Mr. P. Beinhacker, a city planner and architect, and a frequent consultant of the Ministry of Transport from 1969 to 1970, was project manager at Ste. Scholastique. During 1970, he, Hans Blumenfeld, and a few others, were part of an advisory committee set up to advise the government.

Mr. Beinhacker's influence at the Ministry is enormous. He was one of the few who advised against a great new airport, but recommended a system of airports. He was also the man who urged the government to set up a land bank to reduce capital costs on airport construction. Furthermore, it was Mr. Beinhacker who often advised Mr. Jamieson. On some occasions, when the Minister received public delegations, Mr. Beinhacker's presence was very noticeable (he was often called upon to answer some of the difficult questions).

Reliance on planners and outside experts is necessary if the operation of government is to be efficient and effective. But overreliance is something else. The Ministry of Transport has failed to realize that planners and experts have an axe to grind. Sometimes they come up with grandiose schemes and then ask the taxpayers to finance them. As the Metro Roads Commissioner, Sam Cass, once observed, automobile traffic will never get any better because new expressways create the traffic to fill them. Does the same apply to airports?

Hugh Winsor of the *Globe and Mail* has argued convincingly that what is desperately needed is a brand new approach to transportation. There is far too much emphasis on computers, statistics, and projections at the expense of answers to such basic questions as: Should the Ministry of Transport facilitate unlimited growth of air travel? Is charter travel a continuing phenomenon? Are there viable alternatives to air travel? Mr. Winsor feels that it is about time all levels of government not only responded to demand but learned to channel demands. Rescheduling of flights and restructuring of travel habits could eliminate a lot of Malton's problems. There are times of the day when airport use is at a low, and times when the congestion is frightening. Convenient passenger depots, measures to discourage the use of the private car to and from the airport, and the redesigning of facilities could usher in a whole new approach to travel.

To further underline the deficiencies in the federal role from 1969 to early 1972, there was a large turnover of senior officials in the Ministry. A number of them left the public service for more lucrative jobs in the private sector, and a few found the conditions of employment far from conducive to efficiency. One of the negotiators from the province of Ontario pointed out that changes in federal personnel often resulted in a lack of continuity and gave Ontario a bargaining advantage. To compound matters, the federal negotiating team was not a homogeneous body with a consistent plan. Hence, Ontario, not always sure who it was negotiating with (consultants, senior civil servants, or politicians), drove a hard bargain.

The greatest difficulty that faced the federal authorities was the initial attitude that a new airport in Toronto was largely a regional and technical matter. Montreal, Vancouver, and Toronto were important regional centres, and new facilities ensured a national approach.

Overreliance on technical experts posed another set of problems. Technical people work with given quantities. They analyse, clarify, and show the results of processes or decisions, and since the thrust of the federal government was initially technical and legalistic, they came up with technical and legalistic answers. A new Toronto airport is needed; it is our responsibility. Where is the best place to build it?

Despite the establishment of a Department of Urban Affairs, Ottawa has no integrated approach. People within the Ministry of Transport were not working closely with the Department of Urban Affairs. Despite pronouncements to this effect, cross-fertilization has not and will not likely occur in the near future. Government at Ottawa remains highly departmentalized. On the other hand, Ontario, under former Premier Robarts developed a great deal of interdepartmental co-operation. For example, regional planning demanded collaboration between such departments as Municipal Affairs, Treasury, and Trade and Development. Thus, whereas the federal position was comparable to pins on a map, the provincial perspective was broadly linear. To Ontario, growth dynamics is as important as noise, lands and planning and as vital as existence.

2. The Provincial Approach

There is no doubt that the choice of Pickering was largely prompted by Ontario. The federal government as late as 1971 favoured a western site, whereas the province has always preferred an eastern site. When it appeared that the federal government was leaning towards Peters Corner, there were provincial hints of non-co-operation. McKeough pointed out that they would not pay for services which could run as high as $400 million. If the federal government insisted on that site, they would have to pay for all the services. Should an eastern site be chosen, the province was willing to share the cost of services. The transportation corridor provided for in the Toronto Centred Region plan could serve as an access route. The Ontario Water Resources Commission agreed to adjust its York regional sewer and water service so as to meet the needs of the area. Both governments were anxious to avoid a confrontation. The notion of a system of airports allowed the province to have its choice and the federal government to have a western site in the form of an expanded Hamilton and London airport.

What factors were crucial in the choice of Pickering?

• The switch from a single airport to a system of airports meant that sites with four runways could now be considered.
• The province desired to provide economic stimulation for the region east of Metropolitan Toronto.
• Pickering falls within the main east-west transportation route.
• Political concerns: Toronto is too powerful an entity, it has to be contained.

The first three points are self-explanatory and do not necessarily suggest Pickering as a logical choice; another eastern site could have met the requirements. The crux of the whole problem is the fourth point, but like the iceberg much of the explanation is under water.

What were the *political concerns* evident in the choice of Pickering?

(i) *Land speculation.* This was true of almost every site that looked like the most likely. Speculators were active in Beverley township, Orangeville, and Campbellville. However, the intensity of activity in the Pickering area was greater. The proposed Cedarwood community, dating back to 1969, and the ill-fated Century City had created a pitch of speculative activity seldom surpassed. Among the big property holders in Pickering Township were Runnymede

Development Corporation Ltd. (its former Treasurer: Robert Kaplan, Liberal member of Parliament for Don Valley) and Revenue Properties Co. Ltd., which assembled 6000 acres in Uxbridge Township to create Century City. The latter conflicted with the Toronto Centred Region plan and was later disbanded. Some of this land will now become part of the airport site.

Much of the land purchased in the area is shrouded in mystery, but a few factors stand out. Developers have zeroed in on Cedarwood. German money began buying property in the area after 1969. Dalton Bales bought when he was Minister of Labour in 1969. Gordon Carton, M.P.P., incorporated Tona Investments, a land development company owned by Chapman Real Estate.

The following is a list of properties owned by large development corporations in the new Cedarwood area in Markham Township. It is very peculiar that only one property held by Markborough Properties lies within the Airport site, the rest are in the new North-South Expressway to the Airport.

Owner	Location	Assessment Roll No.	Acreage
Markborough Properties Ltd.	Lot 14, 15 Conc. 9	25-7141 & 26-0655	127.30 50.0
Markborough Properties Ltd.	Lot 19, Conc. 9		
Markborough Properties Ltd.	Lot 16-18 Conc. 9	26-0039	80.0
Markborough Properties Ltd.	Lot 14,W½ Conc. 10	25-7518	187.523
Markborough Properties Ltd.	Lot 20, Conc. 10 (in Airport site)	26-2098	93.83

It appears that the south boundary of this airport site was not arbitrarily chosen, but chosen to accommodate certain corporations or individuals.

West German corporation land holdings in Cedarwood, Markham Township, are as follows. (These corporations pay no taxes in Canada on capital gains in real estate.)

Owner	Location	Assessment Roll No.	Acreage
Regin Properties Ltd.	Lot 4, 5, Conc. 10		63
Regin Properties Ltd.	Conc.9	25-2516 & 25-2414 25-0901	426
Regin Properties Ltd.	Lot 4, Conc. 10	25-1537	77
Regin Properties Ltd.	Lot 4, Conc. 10	25-1770	113.28
Von Thurn und Taxis Maria F		25-0281	56.23
Countess Marie Therese von Opersdorff	Lot 3 & 4, Conc.11	25-2093	84.73
Helene Princess von Thurn und Taxis		25-0399	96

It would be informative to know something of the shareholders of the West German companies. One wonders whether there are Canadians holding shares.

Other important shareholders (as of information provided in 1969) are listed in Appendix "A". The approximate total amount of land owned by developers in Markham Township in the area involved in the Airport/Cedarwood site was 2,366 acres; in Pickering Township, 3,432 acres; in Uxbridge Township, 2,249 acres.

One wonders whether there is a correlation between land speculation and the choice of Pickering Airport. One thing is clear: in Ontario, developers are a force to be reckoned with, and some of the companies have made large contributions to some of the political parties. Mr. McKeough's statement that no matter what happens to the Airport, Cedarwood will go ahead is subject to a variety of interpretations.

(ii) *Mr. McKeough.* The role of Mr. McKeough in the Pickering affair is a moot one. During the premiership of John Robarts he was Municipal Affairs Minister. He was able, but far from outstanding. With the accession of William Davis to the premiership, and the reorganization of the government of

Ontario, he became the number-two man and later a super-minister, but without departmental ministerial support.

Under the Davis regime McKeough has emerged as one of the most talented but toughest ministers. He has also earned a reputation for being a good speaker and administrator, marred only by a streak of arrogance and a marked disdain for the opposition and the press. Mr. McKeough is to the Davis team what Robert MacCaulay was to the Frost administration.

It is commonly held that Mr. McKeough was responsible for the choice of Pickering. This is partially true.

Negotiations between Ottawa and Queen's Park were handled by Messrs. McNaughton and Jamieson. However, in December 1971, Mr. McKeough was co-opted. In early 1972 he assumed responsibility for Airport negotiations, but he had little background knowledge of the issues, and moved too quickly in settling the choice of a site. Hence his inept handling of the matter.

Throughout much of the controversy, the Premier of Ontario has been puzzlingly quiet. According to one prominent Conservative, there is an arrangement between Mr. McKeough and Mr. Davis. Had the former succeeded in his onerous job, he would be the natural choice as the next premier — a change which could take place within the next thirty-six months.

It was therefore important that McKeough stand on his own feet and project an image of toughness and decisiveness. Mr. Davis, for his part, would throw the Ontario provincial Conservative party machinery behind Robert Stanfield. Should Stanfield fail to win the election and should a leadership conference be called, Mr. Davis would be a leadership candidate. Pickering Airport was then a political test, particularly for McKeough. By his decisiveness and ability to negotiate with the federal government, McKeough would prove himself capable of the provincial party leadership. Political advancement was tied to it.

For his part, the Premier of Ontario has sought to play a skilful role. His stand on the Pickering Airport is largely dictated by the lesson of Spadina. Originally pro-Spadina, he was surprised at the political windfall he reaped from cancelling the project. His image-makers have now sought to exploit the Spadina decision, by casting him as an exponent of the new politics, as concerned about ecology as he is about the economy. The Davis strategy — and Davis is more of a politician than a statesman — is to sit on the fence and watch the direction in which the political wind is blowing. He does not want to alienate the anti-Airport forces, yet at the same time he is not openly applauding the Pickering site. He tries hard to convey the impression that Pickering is completely Ottawa's choice.

The position of the Premier is also that of the federal Conservatives. For a while Mr. Stanfield refused to make an unequivocal statement on the Pickering Airport, and this gave the Tory candidates a great deal of flexibility. Some align themselves with the anti-Airport movement and others take a pro-Airport stand.

This strategy was put to the test on September 30th and October 2nd, respectively. On September 30th, Robert Stanfield stated in ecology-conscious Toronto that a Conservative government would shelve plans for a new Toronto area airport at Pickering and in its place expand and improve facilities at Malton. "The case for a second airport has not been made," Mr. Stanfield declared. He also stated that while he was willing to listen to contrary opinions, "it would take a lot of persuasion to convince . . .(him) that a second airport . . . needs to be a priority at this time."

Mr. Stanfield indicated, without spelling out details, that Ontario Conservative Premier William Davis agrees with this stand. Referring to the proposed public inquiry announced by Mr. Jamieson, Mr. Stanfield labelled it "a political expedient with a view to getting through the election."

On October 2nd, Michael Starr, a former cabinet minister and now a Conservative candidate in the Oshawa-Whitby riding, took an opposing stand. As a strong supporter of the new proposed airport, he declared, "Everybody is entitled to his own opinion. This is a local issue." Mr. Starr feels that the airport will be an economic boon for his area. He continued, "If there wasn't a need, Mr. Trudeau's government has perpetrated a huge fraud on the people of southern Ontario."

The Pickering airport will create jobs for thousands of people: "Oshawa and Whitby are looking forward and gearing up for the economic boon the airport will bring about."

Meanwhile, Frank McGee, Conservative candidate in adjacent Ontario riding, has spoken against the new airport. He favours converting the site into an industrial park and retaining the surrounding lands for continued agricultural and residential use.

(iii) *The decision.* In our political tradition, policy formation is the responsibility of the minister and cabinet. The experts within government or the consultants from outside may offer advice or provide support or criticism for a given course of action, but ultimate responsibility rests with the government. In the ordinary course of events, policy formation is rarely the result of a set of rational sequential steps, but often the result of a series of "disjointed incremental" measures. In short, policy is often the result of muddling through a situation.

The choice of Pickering fits the "muddling through", or to paraphrase Mr. McKeough's phrase, the "rolling in" model. Rumour has it that the decision on Pickering was made in late 1971. After extensive communication, Messrs. Jamieson and McNaughton met in an Ottawa hotel room, and over some refreshment they agreed to compromise on Pickering.

(iv) *The die was cast!* The fighting response of the community was totally unexpected. To remove the matter from electoral debate, two developments took place.

(a) When airport opponents and concerned environmentalists expressed dismay at building an airport on Class I farm land, the Ministry of Transport worked out a rationalization. It maintained that since much of the land was owned by speculators it was ripe for urbanization anyway. So following the airport announcement a study was commissioned: *Land Dynamics: The Toronto II Airport Study—Land Ownership of Markets—July 7, 1972.*

The sponsors, Environment Canada, instead of investigating the land quality, farming enterprises, ecological significance, and value to Canadians of "a scarce and highly valued resource", followed Transport Canada's argument and "examined ownership and market characteristics" — hardly environmental subjects.

The report concludes that near Markham and Stouffville, along proposed trunk sewers, and in Century City there has indeed been speculation. There was a wave of speculation in late 1971 when a Pickering site was rumoured; "a predominance of corporate ownership is noted in Markham Township north and east of the Town of Markham"; and in the sample area which encompasses 99,000 acres, 24,860.2 are privately held.

One interesting table shows that land prices declined from $2,070 per acre in 1969 to $525 per acre in 1970, apparently due to the announcement of the Toronto Centred Region in May of 1970, interesting evidence that zoning will control speculation and even reverse the upward local price trend. By Autumn of 1971 land prices again began to climb.

The study fails to grapple with the problem of urbanization of Class I lands. It merely illustrates that weak governments which allow or encourage rezoning will also encourage speculation. It does not dispute the fact that the Airport site is Class I land, a valuable and scarce resource which should be preserved.

There is a miserable acceptance of the fact that, if a speculator owns land, the land use should be changed to accommodate the owner. It is an invitation to future speculators to look at Zone 2 (agriculture and recreation) of the Toronto Centred Region Plan with lecherous intent. The sequence is purchase, run prices up, escalate farm taxes, force the farmer out of the area and apply for rezoning.

The report is not entirely without hope. It also shows that if zoning is applied, prices will drop and the land can be preserved.

(b) On September 1, 1972, Mr. Jamieson announced in the House of Commons that "the Government has decided there should be public hearings and that they will be conducted by an independent inquiry."

It is intriguing to note that this announcement was made the day Mr. McKeough resigned from the Ontario Cabinet. One wonders whether there was a correlation between the departure of the Minister and the federal announcement. Had Mr. McKeough been in office he would certainly have argued against it.

One knowledgeable reporter was convinced that from the Ministry of Transport's point of view, a few embarrassing stories would cut the Ontario government down to size, and thus make the federal role much easier.

6. People or Planes

Helen Auld finished putting the cuttings into the earth
she had prepared by sifting it through the screen and
adding a little peat moss. These were the last of the cuttings she would put in this spring. Meanwhile, she would
prepare the flats for the pansy seeds for putting them out
as early in the spring as she could. The greenhouse she
had made in the corner of the living room was full of
colour as the primulas blossomed purple on one side and
the daffodils she had forced showed yellow on the other.

She and John, her husband, looked forward to the spring
when they could get back to their flower garden and watch
for the new tulips they had put in last fall.

She looked out over the snowbank to where the tulip
bed lay beneath the huge drift which had approached the
bottom of the bird-feeding station. Two jays were busy
gorging themselves on the sunflower seeds that had been
put out earlier. Meanwhile, the chickadees were eating at
their smaller station.

The house was small. Just big enough for her retired
husband and herself — a happy spot to spend the rest of
their lives. On its walls were pictures of the original
house that had been built by the Barclays, her great-
grandparents, in the early nineteenth century. But Helen
had not come back to the house until fairly recently. Her
duties as a nurse had kept her in the city. Now these

duties were over and she had returned to her ancestral home.

Unlike her great grandmother who had imported flowers and strange shrubs from Scotland, Helen usually grew native plants — the roses, asters, delphiniums, and nigellas which did so well in the rich soil that surrounded the cottage. Even now she could make out the grotesque shapes that the snow had made about the burlapped rosebushes. Soon they would be uncovered to blossom all summer long in the hot sun.

But before that could happen there was the matter of an airport. She began to prepare an early supper so that she would be at the meeting on time.

It is a truism that we are living at a critical point in history. Problems abound that make daily living precarious. The world is, as it were, caught up in a giant whirlpool and we are desperately fighting for survival.

For a while it would seem that man is in harness and events are in the driver's seat; technocracy has become the order of the day. Nothing is small or simple — indeed the scale of intricacy that envelops political, economic, and technical life baffles the ordinary citizen. Technical reports, team studies, feasibility undertakings, government designs, and development plans are all geared to tell us what is good for us or in our best interests. Ours is an age of technical experts, one in which the system or the scheme seems more important than the individual or his community.

With or without opposition, technocracy extends its dogged octopus-like tentacles to all areas of life. It deports itself as the monarch of all it surveys — there is no one to dispute its claims. With enormous powers of coercion, it prefers to gain our co-operation by appealing to the myth of scientific or technological progress. Science is no longer viewed as part of the search for understanding, but the quest for power.

In recent years there has been a resurgence of a world-wide community movement challenging technocracy and social engineering and defying bureaucracy and social injustices. People are no longer prepared to be relegated to impotence, trampled on, treated like a statistic or like a cog in a great machine. They want to return to a system where there is government by, not just for, the people and where life, liberty, and property are adequately protected. Admittedly some instances of protest are petty, but what is significant is the renewed conviction that action can effect changes. The right of a community to ask for a change of announced policy is an inalienable right, and the basis of government to accede to "the consent of the governed" is an irrefutable principle of democracy.

The dream of our thinkers has been a society so formed that the sentiments and roles of communities can be integrated into a national will; where participation and direction are not viewed as alternatives, but two sides of the same coin; and where history is not viewed as static but as a dynamic interplay between the past and the present − the past is revealed in the present, and the present concealed in the past. Participatory democracy, if such is not a cliché, must mean more than freedom from arbitrary power or the tyranny of the magistrate. It must mean the liberation and development of the individual's potential, the protection and orderly development of the community, and the reorganization of social goals, so that our institutions are nurtured to reflect humanistic values and the best philosophic ideals.

The great Anglo-American philosopher Alfred North Whitehead wrote: "Mankind is now in one of its rare moods of shifting its outlook. The mere compulsion of tradition has lost its force." Indeed, the mood of shifting outlook is here. Growing social awareness has resulted in new pressures being exerted on the political system to undertake programs of physical and social renewal. To large numbers the ecology of our world is more important than the gross national product, and the quality of life more vital than longevity or the material dimension. If man is a social animal, if there is a correlation between the individual and the community, and if it is not life that is to be chiefly desired but the good life, then what is needed is a new concern, a new venture of the human spirit.

To the people of Pickering Township the prime purpose of the projected airport is not to facilitate or increase the possibilities of human association, social intercourse, or choice but to increase physical movement. By itself, maximum speed of traffic has very little significance. The process that has been undermining our transportation is the elimination of all but motor vehicles and jet planes. Such a trend is not a technological advance; it is what one scientist called "de-building." De-building is the substitution of artificial measures for natural age-old process — a break in the source of connection that men have long felt with their environment. In a sense it is a supreme manifestation of alienation and identity confusion. A good illustration appeared in an editorial in the *Globe and Mail* on April 12, 1972: "The province has an airport site, but not really just where it wanted it. Ottawa has chosen the site, but not where the federal government wanted it. The people of Pickering have an airport site and they don't want it."

The real problem is that to many residents of the area the choice is clear — a new airport and the destruction of an historic community, or a relocation — rejection of an unnecessary airport and the preservation of a way of life. In a way the community feels that it is being subjected to a "long train of abuses and usurpations" and that its vital interests are being sacrificed.

The challenge mounted by POP and by people across this country has not gone unnoticed. Canadians from all walks of life have expressed their opinions: in newspapers, magazines, submissions, petitions — and in graffiti on the washroom walls at Malton.

An explosive publication, prepared by the Town Planning Institute of Canada, is included in Appendix B of this text.

The Reaction of the Press

The first announcement of the airport filled the newspapers with maps showing what area would be taken by the airport and by Cedarwood City. The initial reaction of People or Planes was a series of meetings which rapidly generated

73

news. A massive meeting in Pickering on March 18 received coverage by all the media, and the campaign was on.

The *Toronto Star* was late in publishing an editorial comment. It was not until April 29 that a major article appeared. Captioned "A convincing case for second airport", it read in part: "The Star believes the federal government has made a convincing case for building a second international airport to serve the Toronto region. Admittedly the persuasiveness of the argument made in documents and studies by the Department of Transport this week depends on forecasting of passenger loads up until the end of the century. And in statistical forecasting, to further the 'horizon', that is, the longer the future period to be covered the more uncertain the predictions become."

The editorial claimed that the forecasting could be valid to 1980, but the forecasts were much less dependable beyond 1980 to the year 2000. It then commented that there could be technological breakthroughs that would significantly change the picture. "If the assumptions of passenger loads are right, then there are only two options: Enlarge Malton or build another airport. The federal government, with the backing of the provincial cabinet, has decided on a second airport. The Star believes that decision is the right one."

The editorial went on to point out that *if* there were a technical breakthrough in ground transportation and *if* passengers could be kept from going to the airport and *if* the load projections were out of line and *if* the noise levels would be accepted by people around Malton, *then* we would not need a second airport.

By May 24 (after Prime Minister Trudeau had said there would be no public inquiry into the need for a second airport), the *Star* acknowledged the arguments of Barney Danson, M.P. for York North, and stated:

A hearing should be held. Even if it is unlikely to produce the sort of evidence that would alter the government's decision, it would give the airport opponents a democratic outlet.

In England, when the government decided on a new airport for London, a series of sites was proposed and public hearings held by a commission on all of them. In the end, the Conservative government chose an east coast location which was not the commission's first choice.

The public was made fully aware of the arguments for and against each site so there was no suggestion that individual rights were being trampled by an unfeeling state. Transportation Minister Don Jamieson says that technique was not available in Canada—speculators would have moved in on any site mentioned if the government had not kept its choice secret until the last moment.

But that is all the more reason why a hearing should be made possible now. The *Star* believes Ottawa's case for a second airport—backed by Queen's Park—is a convincing one. But it is by no means air tight. It is simply the wisest decision to make on the information available . . . But the opponents should not have to depend entirely on their own resources to develop their counter-arguments and get them before the public. They are entitled to a public hearing.

But by July 17 there had once again been a change in the main direction of editorial thought: "Give the airport enquiry a chance," said the editorial. It then offered a hearing under the Expropriation Act rather than a public inquiry. (The Expropriation Act does not provide any facility for a public inquiry. It, by law, registers objections and passes them on to the Minister of Public Works.)

Probably many foes of the airport will not be satisfied with these public expropriation hearings. They will point out that the people appointed to conduct the hearings only pass on objections and advice to the government. The government can still ignore the hearings and take the land it wants anyway.

To give in to this kind of thinking is to consider the government of Canada one vast conspiracy to thwart the will of the citizens. We happen to believe that in Ottawa and Queen's Park there are men of independent spirit who can change their minds if they are given good reason to do so. The safeguards built into expropriation proceedings give opponents of the airport many opportunities to make their case before the government and before the public. They can also go to court to challenge the prices offered by the federal government.

But the *Globe and Mail* apparently had some suspicions of those who were running the country. On April 12 it commented:

It has taken more than three years for the Ontario government to admit that those long negotiations with Ottawa on a new international airport for Toronto weren't about an airport at all. They were about location. Queen's Park evidently knew nothing, asked nothing, about airport plans and use.

Ontario bought a location ... The province has an airport site but not really just where it wanted it. Ottawa has chosen the site but not where the federal Government wanted it. The people of Pickering have an airport site and they don't want it.

It is difficult to believe that a provincial Government could commit itself to spending millions of the taxpayers' money without knowing what it is to be spent on, what use the airport is to be put to, what need there is for a second airport, how much will have to be spent to make the idea a viable reality.

By April 25 the *Globe* had picked up a statement by Jamieson and used it as the background for an editorial. The statement made on a broadcast and later in a speech read, "It would be criminally negligent on the part of the federal authorities not to make provision for other facilities for Toronto by the year 1979-1980."

The editorial pointed out that

The country is entirely dependent on Mr. Jamieson's research in this matter, can only take it on trust. But trust has to be related to performance.

The performance that can be expected at Pickering may be measured against the performance which is at present being provided by the same people at Montreal's new international airport at Ste. Scholastique. . . .

They are not reports to cheer Ontario for it will be the very same people who are producing Ste. Scholastique who will be working on the Pickering airport; and indeed that is one of the things that concerns the airlines. They don't want to have to work out of two impossible airports.

Other pages in the *Globe and Mail* echoed scepticism. Scott Young in a series of brilliant columns brought great comfort to the beleaguered people of Pickering. In "A call for protest" he said:

I hereby enlist as a spear-carrier in the ranks of those who believe that the proposed Pickering airport is grounds for certifying the federal Cabinet which proposed it, and the provincial Cabinet which approved it, as insane.

The only possible support must come from (a) those who want to benefit financially; and (b) the gravel pit operators whose ugly scars in the area now will seem scarcely worthy of mention in comparison to this infinitely vaster sin against nature.

I hope that opposition to this affront against common sense eventually will be nationwide, the largest single protest movement in Canadian history. It should be. It can be. This issue has everything: a senseless expenditure of tax money, a mindless destruction of grass and trees and hills and vales, the killing of a beloved way of life for many thousands, and an inhuman paving over and befouling. . . .

. . . To build a new airport now would be a modern example of the same blindness that led railroad builders of earlier times to build huge temples of railroad stations.

Every city in North America now has these white elephants, many of them nearly empty and useless. The railroad tracks themselves were needed at the time but not terminals on that scale. The situation in air travel is the reverse: the terminals are needed, but in the future many runways on the present scale will not be essential, let alone any need to build whole new airports and multiply the future waste. . . .

Politicians – there is the answer. The federal Liberals are about to ask us to re-elect them. Every candidate who supports this crime against the countryside should be rejected at the polls. In a country that does need many things – better housing, more parks, more recreational facilities, better pensions for the elderly – it should be a national issue. They should be forced by public opinion to back down and forget it.

The *Globe and Mail* editorial page kept pounding away at "airport shortcomings." On June 12 it stated that government-released reports did not support the statement that Pickering satisfy the requirements for a general economic stimulus in the eastern corridor.

In other words an airport four miles from Metro when coupled with a new community of 200,000 will do little to discourage growth in Metro Toronto. It will, in fact, only add another immense and expanding suburb. . . .

Why has the Ontario government decided to so weaken its chances of making regional development work?

Young continued to press the issue. In "The hard way" he explored the mechanics by which Mr. Paul Hellyer had decided not to enlarge the Malton Airport. In particular, he picked up the dilemma of Barney Danson who three years previously had been in favour of expansion at Malton but now had an irate group of ratepayers in his riding who

opposed the Pickering venture. He pointed out Danson's
popularity after the Malton expansion had been put off, and
said:

They weren't hurt by the fact that Barney Danson had been a leading
campaigner for Paul Hellyer both in Toronto and in his losing fight for
the Liberal leadership. Anyway, they won. It must have been a heady
moment for Mr. Danson in his first few months as a politician (elected
in June that year). Heady, that is, while he was saying Goodby Malton.
Not quite so heady six weeks ago when he was saying, Hello
(gasp) . . . Pickering?

Later in the month he characterized the proposed new
airport a "Basic boondoggle." In the column he pointed out
that, on October 1, 1968,

. . . John Baldwin, then deputy minister of transport, informed the
press in Toronto that the department had all but abandoned plans for
a second airport, because expansion at Malton would handle traffic
nicely until beyond 1985. This expert judgment had dictated the
position of the transport minister of the time, Paul Hellyer, and even
in 1970 Mr. Jamieson was saying that the Malton expansion was one of
his options.
    Question: What happened? Answer: Politics . . .
    Mr. Jamieson should answer these questions: . . . Are we so short of
legitimate requirements in other fields that we must seek out illegiti-
mate ones — when the cost itself is a national concern affecting all
taxpayers? Have we so much land for green space and recreation use
near Toronto that we can squander tens of thousands of acres on
aeronautical impulse-buying?

While the snow had departed from the fields of Pickering
by May 3, it was still on Young's mind. On that day he
pointed out in a column, "Bank of snow jobs", that

In contemplating Ontario Superminister Darcy McKeough's sensa-
tional new plans for a concrete green belt around Toronto, with the
proposed Pickering airport to be the first thorn in its crown, I am
sometimes afflicted by the ennui that I hear is part of drowning, or
freezing to death. I am going down for the third time in a sea of
technocrats. I am freezing in a snowbank of snow jobs. . . .
    If Toronto International indeed will reach the Department of
Transport estimate of 30 million passengers by 1990, why, eureka,
that will be as many as Chicago's O'Hare handles now in 1972! So why
not just make Toronto International as big, over the next 18 years, as
O'Hare is now?

And: If Cedarwood, or North Pickering, or Bigger-and-Better-Brougham, today has the 200,000 citizens who are said to be in its future, would anybody now be planning a new airport in its immediate neighborhood?...

And remember from the federal side all the second airport arguments are brought to you by the same people who built the airport at Gander (That's G-a-n-d-e-r, madam. It's in Newfoundland. I know you've never heard of it, or landed there.)

Each regular position put forward by the government was countered by Young. He pointed out in a column headed "Activist Rascals":

The Transport Minister himself was talking to the annual meeting of the York Scarborough Liberal Association. He was quoted in the Toronto Star as criticizing citizen groups that attempt to block government decisions. "They have a right to be heard," the Star reported Mr. Jamieson as saying, "but they must respect the responsibility of elected officials to make a decision ultimately. Otherwise nothing will be done and the future will overtake us." ... The fact that the obstructionist rascals cover a lot of territory was pointed out last week-end when a festival on the airport site ran out of anti-airport petition forms.

In another column he wrote:

There is scarcely a single element in the plans for a second Toronto area airport that cannot be shot down easily if the matter is approached in the manner it deserves – a parliamentary inquiry, investigation and debate. ... Why should the public accept a steam-roller decision that comes from the same people who told us in 1968 that Malton expansion was better than a second airport?

In "The airport issue: some new ideas" Young noted the comments of an Air Canada pilot and pointed out several solutions to the terminal problem at Malton. The column ended:

None of what he is proposing is beyond present technology. It is the sort of solution that should be sought instead of taking an easy out, as the government did, of throwing up their hands and saying, "OK, Charlie, bulldoze us 18,000 acres and lets build another airport."

By June 21 he was examining more closely the Cedarwood City proposition. This saw the province expropriating land in

order to build a housing community. The land would no
necessarily be developed by the province but could be turned
over to a private developer for their profit. In the "Roots of
dismay", Young said:

When Keith and Mavis Walton drove last night from their Scarborough
hardware store to their place north of Pickering, they had the feeling
they had had for three months; that machinery was underway to gyp
them out of what was rightfully theirs.

Gyp, as plain as that, and no honeyed words from hired PR guns
will change it.

They know their 50½ acres would work out to between 90 and 100
building lots in the super suburb the government wants to build in that
area. "If it happens, some private developer will make a good profit
from it, you can be sure of that," Keith said. "Who gets all the money?
Into whose pocket does it go?"

It doesn't help that the Ontario government refuses a public
inquiry into the matter of an airport and new city in the region (as
does the federal government). This only increases the suspicion in the
Waltons and people like them that the government has no answers that
would stand up to such an inquiry.

The lead editorial on August 11 in the *Globe and Mail* was
along the same lines.

Until now this province and its municipalities and other agencies have
been very reluctant, and rightly reluctant, to make it possible for land
to be expropriated from one private individual or company to be
resold to another private individual or company. [Referring to an
amendment to the Housing Development Act which had been passed
on June 27.] This amendment would not even seem to require that it
be sold, that there is a return to the provincial treasury; land could,
"as the Minister may determine", be "otherwise disposed of"; it
could, one is left to suspect, be handed out to favored developers as
grants. . . .

It does give a property owner a certain feeling of insecurity. It does
make him wonder if all that reform of expropriation legislation,
prompted by the McRuer Report on Civil Rights, had any permanent
value.

Another columnist, Gary Lautens, had devoted his May 9
column in the *Star* to the airport matter. However, he had
used it more for irony than as a committed piece of writing.
He pointed out that "nobody wants a superhighway within
50 miles of his own backyard", therefore the decision to
build an airport creates a serious problem.

To be perfectly fair to all taxpayers we've decided to blacktop the entire province," a spokesman at Queen's Park revealed.

"Why do you want to do that?" I asked.

"So we can change the location of expressways, jetports, access roads and truck routes every few weeks," was his reply.

However, Lautens' interlocutor's brilliant scheme for paving the whole province had to be held up until: "As soon as we can get delivery of 865,974,229,540 traffic lights."

Many writers used the airport as a base for humorous sketches. The Stouffville *Tribune* had an article that dealt with the problems the federal government faced in trying to place a runway without causing excessive noise over any of the surrounding built-up areas. The federal government's solution was the "kinky runway". This was a runway that was curved back and forth so that aircraft noise would not intrude on Stouffville, Dixon's Hill, or Uxbridge. According to the author it was successful in the matter of noise. However, many of the pilots found some difficulties in landing and taking off in a zig-zag manner.

The Markham *Economist and Sun*, in addition to a strong editorial campaign against the airport and particularly against Cedarwood City, had several humorous comments. Landowners who rapidly became vocal in the campaign were the "uncompensated losers". These were people who lived on the periphery of the airport, were not going to be expropriated, and would receive only noise and decrease of land values as the result of the airport. This group was satirized in a Robin Hood theme article as "Uncompensated Boozers".

But a great deal of serious writing was carried on as well. In particular, a series of articles by Tom Coleman in the *Globe and Mail*, June 12 and 15, represented a high point of investigative reporting. This type of reporting was carried on well by the *Globe and Mail*, but the *Star* seemed content to work from hand-outs given to them by the government.

The articles examined the question of whether Toronto should have two major airports and compared transportation problems in this region with those in the United States. They ended with serious doubts as to the forecasts of aircraft movements that had been made by the government team and

the ability of the government to channel the passengers to
one or other airport. They were also concerned with the
multi-million-dollar cost of providing roads and mass-transit
links between downtown and the new airport. Citing exam
ples from Winnipeg, Montreal, and Edmonton, the article
concluded that, "the passengers and the airlines, in the fina
analysis, are the ones who decide whether or not an airpor
works. And both the passengers and the airlines, in the case o
Chicago's O'Hare and most other major world airports have
emphatically shown that they are more than willing to put up
with long delays for take-off, harrassed, over-crowded and
expensive parking and ticketing arrangements, jammed res
taurants and bars just for the convenience and flexibility o
being where the action is." Coleman made it obvious that he
considered the action would remain at Malton Airport long
after any second Toronto International Airport had been
built.

Arnold Edinborough, writing in his column in the *Financial Post*, headlined his comments, "It takes a peculiar talent
– to make airports so badly". He pointed out that the
proposed new airport at Pickering would take an incredible
amount of money to connect it with the centre it is supposed
to serve.

The airlines aren't happy with our airports, and the people who fly on
those airlines aren't happy with those airports.
   Why, then, do we go on using airports as political footballs instead
of facilities for people?
   Perhaps it is because just the people have moved into the air age –
the politicians and their civil servants have not yet arrived there.

With the noise that was being raised in Toronto and
surrounding area by the POP group, it was inevitable that
areas across Canada would begin to hear the sounds. In order
to help this along, POP sent a letter to all newspapers in
Canada alerting them to the proposed waste of tax dollars for
a white-elephant airport which would benefit only "fat cat"
Toronto and would do nothing to help the regional disparities
which existed across the country.

The Kemptville, Nova Scotia, *Advertiser* editorialized:

While regional jealousies could easily be excited by such a situation, here is another point which concerns everyone who helps to foot the federal bills.

For two big new projects to work on, Ottawa will have almost unlimited opportunities to design something even worse and even more expensive than Malton.

On April 29th, the Thunder Bay *Times Journal* stated:

Secrecy will benefit no-one. A new international airport is too expensive and has too much effect on the environment to emerge from a cloud of secret studies. If a public hearing is not to be held, then each and every study must be made available at least to the protest groups, and there must be time allowed for study.

Two days later *The London Free Press* stated:

In his determined defense of the Pickering site for Toronto's second airport, Transport Minister Donald Jamieson ignored a major objection to it. More than two million people who live west of Toronto will have to travel through and around metro to use the new airport. But the name of the game is not to put an airport in a location which will spark economic expansion in underdeveloped areas. Prime development is desirable of course. There is only trouble ahead, however, when an airport like the one proposed for Pickering is moved from where it should be in order to try to develop a backwater area. If Pickering needs development it should be encouraged by tax concessions, land assembly by the Provincial Government or by other inducements to industry. Distorting the province's air and other transport system to achieve development of a specific tract of land is an abuse of the planner's function. If the answer is that frequent, fast, rapid transit service is to be built between Toronto and Pickering response is obvious. That rapid transit system would be more efficient and serve double the present and future population if it were built westward so that it would serve non-airport transit needs between Toronto and Hamilton, the Kitchener areas and London as well as Malton Airport and the new airport.

The main support from political figures came from Mr. Jamieson and Mr. McKeough who on several occasions pointed out the absolute necessity and wisdom of the choice. However, there was little comment from other members of the federal Cabinet. Opposition was sparked by John Diefenbaker, who in the early days of the decision drew attention to the lack of need and lack of concern with regard to environmental impact. (Mr. Diefenbaker had had his primary school education at Greenwood – in a school house which is now serving as POP's headquarters.)

Paul Hellyer, former Liberal Cabinet member, Action Canada leader, and now Conservative, was reported in the *Globe and Mail*, June 28, as saying: "The choice of Pickering as a site for the proposed airport was a 'monumental blunder that will guarantee a continuation of the uncontrolled urban sprawl around Metro. . . . Malton Airport could be renovated to handle air traffic until the mid-eighties."

George Hees, Minister of Transport before Hellyer, made similar comments in and out of the House.

This hardening of opinions caused Darcy McKeough to comment in the *Star* that the government's task is to "get on with this job and not fiddle faddle around forever". When E Sargent (Liberal, Grey-Bruce) inquired about the cost of the airport in the community of North Pickering, he was accused of "nit-picking". Sargent responded, "Who needs the airport in the first place? Nit-picking my eye, why don't you grow up?"

The paper war spread to other areas. Captain J.D Gallagher, president of the Canadian Association of Airline Pilots, was quoted in the newsletter of the Central Ontario Regional Development Council, July 12, 1971, as saying "What are we going to do with an airport fifty miles out of Toronto? There appears to be no need for a second airport for many years."

This sentiment was echoed by Captain J.R. Desmarais in *Canadian Aviation*, June 1972:

In that celebrated slip of the tongue some 15 years ago, the late C.D Howe said: "What's a million?" It's nothing, of course, but C.D., who ran a bit ahead of the pack, had shown a lack of political tact.

This time, accompanying the announcement of a new airport for Toronto, the underlying question seemed to be: "What's a billion?" But the news was presented in slick fashion, with the bally-hoo which usually accompanies such announcements. To the average man, the expenditures appeared warranted.

In a world of increasingly complex technology, it has become almost impossible for anyone to understand what is going on in any science-related area. The average man's field of vision is limited to his own occupation and, perhaps, to a leisure-time pursuit.

But the political structure which is threaded throughout our technological world is not immune to this lack of knowledge. It has recourse to a team of experts, of course, but if it "doctors" their figures to suit its own purposes, it may find itself very much out on a limb. For outside of the political structure, the particular technology also has its own experts. If to them are added government technocrats in partial contradiction regarding a certain project, a group which feels itself unjustly threatened, and newspapermen who dig deep enough, then the project's credibility becomes questionable.

The proposed new Toronto airport at Pickering, Ont. smacks of an unholy alliance between the federal and provincial governments, a joint machination for the political gain of both. Using the new Montreal Airport at Ste. Scholastique as a partial smokescreen, quoting figures which are disputable, ignoring facts of transportation technology, the governments proudly announced a billion-dollar expenditure of the taxpayers' money.

The airport is unneeded.

This opinion was answered with "equal time" in the next issue of *Canadian Aviation* by the Airport Planning Team. Their message reiterated the previous government documentation.

Strangely enough there was little official comment from the airlines, the International Air Transport Association, or the Air Transport Association of Canada. Mr. Jamieson had been asked to table communications from the airlines regarding the Pickering Airport when POP had visited in Ottawa. However, no information was presented. B.O.A.C. had not made any formal statements, but in a televised interview Mr. Reynolds, the General Manager, pointed out the enormous costs that would result from a split operation between Malton and Pickering. These costs, he pointed out, would greatly increase airline-operating costs and would be unpalatable to the airlines.

The fight continued on many levels. Several attempts were made to weaken the case against the airport by pointing out that the opposition to it was composed of wealthy landowners who were self-seeking in their arguments.

"Opposition to airport is selfish and hysterical", said a letter to the editor in the Toronto *Star*, April 25. A further letter pointed out that the airport hysteria was unwarranted. 'Some residents of the periphery of the new airport certainly have real cause for concern. However, that hysteria being created by some groups is somewhat unwarranted." Furthe comment along this line appeared in a letter in the *New Advertiser*, June 29. This said in part: "Discover the facts and the potential for yourselves, evaluate the sensationalism and emotionalism that is being stirred up against this airport and don't just be a follower. Make your choice and work fo it. Remember, most of the objectors are secure, comfortabl people with 'Do Not Disturb' on their little domain."

That "little domain" seemed to contain something o value to those who lived there. Originally the governmen reports had pointed out that from an agricultural standpoin there was no real land value that would be lost to the airport This caused many letters from residents who quoted bushel of grain taken and amount of butter fat produced.

Mrs. Pat Bouck, of the Pickering Township Environmenta Advisory Committee, pointed out the tremendous loss attendant to the airport in a letter to the *Star*, March 16:

I would like to point out to residents outside the area and in Toront that if the plan goes through to expropriate 68,000 acres of Pickerin, Township land for a new airport, the majority of which is classe Grade 1 agricultural land – the best there is, you will soon be missin, the many benefits of a country area within easy access to the city.

The decision was dropped like a bomb on the area and our electe representatives were given at the most two hours warning. I wonder i the decision to place the airport here was reached with equal haste The proposed 200,000 community of Cedarwood will be in a Nois Exposure Forecast 30 zone which is termed uninhabitable.

I hope we can stop the airport and the tragedy accompanying it.

Another letter to the *Globe and Mail*, signed by Robert G Almack, Claremont, pointed out the tremendous contribu tion the area made to recreation for the citizens of Toronto

More important is the effect on the urban dweller – people from Toronto, Oshawa, etc.: "Scenic attractions in the 10 surrounding Conservation Areas, within a 10-mile radius, are threatened by the location and construction activity of new routes and facilities servicing the airport. People seeking solitude from their urban environment in parks and conservation areas will also be adversely affected by these surrounding service developments."

The most frequented of the 10 Conservation Parks are Bruce's Mills, Greenwood, and Claremont. (Bruce's Mills is six miles from the ite, Greenwood, two and Claremont, 1.5). These areas provide a recreational haven for thousands of Metro residents. In 1970 nearly one-quarter million people visited Bruce's Mills, the same year 72,766 went to Greenwood and 22,594 escaped to Claremont.

The Rouge River, the West Duffins and the East Duffins Creek flow through the airport site. The East Duffins flows through the Claremont and Greenwood Conservation Parks. The following are quotations from the study, which clearly illustrate the effects on these parks:

"These tributaries (Duffins Creek) would be greatly affected by silt generated during construction. If excess silt is picked up by the creek during construction it would dispense downstream, thereby affecting water quality, reducing the capacity of storage reservoirs, blocking culverts and increasing flood hazards significantly.

"Apart from silt pollution, stream quality would also suffer during the construction phase from accidental spills of gas and oil, and chemicals such as calcium chloride (a dust-control chemical which would enter the water course through runoff.) These materials would eventually enter the main tributaries of Duffins Creek and cause further problems downstream." (i.e. Claremont and Greenwood Conservation Parks).

In a letter to the *Globe and Mail*, March 8, Linda Sheppard of Toronto stated:

I'm writing to offer my "congratulations" to Donald Jamieson and Darcy McKeough on their decision to ruin one of the most valuable and attractive hinterland areas of Metro Toronto. Such a decision could be made only by those who do not live permanently in this over-populated area and who do not look for their recreation to public access land within a comfortable day's driving distance. Unfortunately these two qualifications do apply to many of us, the inhabitants of this city.

Having lived in the east end of Toronto, I have many times enjoyed excursions to the country and to the Metro Conservation areas now to be obliterated by "progress". I have observed them to be well used both in winter and summer. I admit, of course, that there are other Conservation areas — those which involve many miles of city driving before the countryside is reached and those which are so crowded that cars are turned away on warm summer days. What compensations are offered for the loss of these facilities? Jet planes? Pollution? A new city? 200,000 people?

T.A. Strike of Greenwood in a letter to the *Star*, May 16, was more direct. He pointed out that he had difficulty in reading the government publication *Three Steps to Tomorrow* which mentioned the loss of precious farmland to scattered developments. "Such concern is hard to credit when precious Pickering is to be savaged, chewed and then McKeoughed." Although the government published a report showing the impact on the environment, it satisfied neither POP nor Stephen Lewis of the N.D.P. Speaking in the Legislative Committee on the 1972-3 estimates for the Department of Environment, he accused Minister James Auld of "supporting the proposed Pickering airport without investigating how it would affect people in noise, water and land pollution. The charge was laid by N.D.P. Leader Stephen Lewis after Mr. Auld admitted his department had had only 'partial input' in the Ontario-Ottawa decision to build second international airport in Pickering" (*Star*, April 18).

But the effect on the environment was only of secondary interest to John Slinger writing in "Across the Nation" in the *Globe and Mail*, May 27. He pointed out in some quarters the Pickering airport looked like a sweet deal. A person who sells his house now could live in the house rent-free over the next two years. When rents for houses in the city are running up to $250 a month it is not difficult to see that a person who sells now can save between $5,000 and $9,000 a year.

This sweetening came little more than a week after the federal Government pulled a move that would delight lovers of chess and streetfighting. The Meadowvale Gambit.

Meadowvale is a speck of a town about ten miles west of Malton but is on the glidepath of an east-west runway at Toronto International Airport. The people there have been complaining about noise from aircraft and an agent of Donald Jamieson's Transport Ministry went to a public meeting and told them that the best solution, in the long run was for them to write Ottawa and say how important the new airport in Pickering is going to be. Anybody who believed this "would serve the public interest by saying so," said the agent.

The *Financial Post* alerted its readers in Arnold Edinborough's column of May 27 to the "sweet deal".

What has really happened is that fast buck developers around Malton Airport have sold cheap land to build houses. They have then petitioned the government to cut down the traffic at the airport because of the houses built near it.

Knuckling as always to such developers, the government now intends to build a new airport instead of stopping the noise. Thus the

Ontario Government is committed to building similar peripheral residential areas near the new airport!

Land use and speculation was not a big factor in the opening days of the argument. However, as the proponents put forth their claims, the presence of Cedarwood beside the proposed airport loomed larger and larger. Attention was focused on the plans of the Ontario government to expropriate for the new city by the passage in the House on June 27 by Attorney-General Dalton Bales of an act to amend the Housing Development Act. This prompted the *Globe and Mail* on August 11 to editorialize in "An unexpected bulldozer":

> Until now this province and its municipalities and other agencies have been very reluctant, and rightly reluctant, to make it possible for land to be expropriated from one private individual or company. This amendment would not even seem to require that it be sold, that there be a return to the Provincial Treasury; land could "as the Minister may determine", be "otherwise disposed of"; it could, one is left to suspect, be handed out to favoured developers as grants.

Land and land deals assume greater and greater importance to the airport question with the revelations concerning Mr. Bales, Mr. Carton, and Mr. McKeough.

The press coverage dropped considerably during the late summer months. There had been exhaustion of information available. However, with the release of two hundred government documents to People or Planes through their lawyer, John J. Robinette, once again articles showed up in the newspapers. Many of these did little to add new information. The battle-line had been drawn and with minor changes solidified. "Don't count on Pickering before it's hatched", wrote Ian Hamer in the Whitby *Review*, August 23. This article brought the argument up to date:

> One of MP Norman Cafik's wiser comments on the results of his recent survey on the proposed second Toronto International Airport was that he would "not oppose the airport being located in Pickering Township, provided it is needed in the first instance."
>
> As Clark Muirhead of Uxbridge has consistently pointed out, "the first instance" in this case was the December 1968 decision by the

then Minister of Transport Paul Hellyer to bow to strong complaints by some Malton-area residents about threats of increased noise; to set a future limit on air traffic through the Malton complex of 12 million passengers per annum; and to find a site, external to Metro, where a second international airport could be brought into service about 1980.

Of the few skeptics questioning the decision at that time, none is known to have resided in Mr. Cafik's riding or to have joined the delegation Mayor Desmond Newman led to Ottawa in the spring of 1969 to seek the regional economic benefits of having the new airport located in this area.

Had the governmental studies since 1969 been conducted openly as is common in other countries – or even in line with the Federal Minister of Transport's policy on consultation – the present situation would probably not have arisen.

Specifically, by early 1970, the governments were forced by "the magnitude of the costs associated with these external sites," (Scugog was one of the four 'finalists'), to return to evaluation of Malton as the main long-range hub of the Toronto Area Airports System.

Professional reports submitted in August and September of that year clearly indicated the feasibility and desirability of such a course and, if made public at that time would have stimulated valuable debate and refinement of the future process of decision-making.

The "guerrilla warfare" engaged in since the (pre-election?) Pickering-Cedarwood announcement of March 2nd has shown that successive salvos of government press releases, reports and ministerial statements cannot silence the "POP-guns" of those immediately affected.

More significantly, newspapers such as the Globe and Mail and Financial Post; government advisors, such as Dr. Omand Solondt former Chairman of the Science Council; aviation bodies, such as IATA and the Air Transport Associations of Canada; and politicians such as John Diefenbaker, Paul Hellyer, Barney Danson and Stephen Lewis have strongly questioned the validity of the two-airport proposition.

A recent formal submission to the two governments from the 300-member Central Ontario Chapter of the Town Planners Institute of Canada admirably sums up the professional point of view.

The warning for Whitbyites in all of this is, surely, "Don't count on Pickering before it's hatched." Political judgements are slowly coming into balance with social, economic and technological evaluations, to assure continued development of the Malton facilities to proper operating levels, i.e., over twice the limits set in 1968.

This would allow up to five years for truly systematic definition of the need for any further major airports, such as Pickering, in the Toronto Centred Region Plan, with actual construction not being required before the mid 1980s. Local expectations as to "benefits" should be tempered by that prospect.

On the other hand, should the governments insist on forging ahead now, with expropriation and construction in Pickering Township, the economic prospect for Whitby and adjacent communities is no better.

The Town Planning Institute brief, referred to above, observes that: "the proposed airport at North Pickering is likely if anything to stimulate development adjacent to and relating to Metropolitan Toronto, rather than in the areas further east."

This would become apparent during the construction phase and be confirmed during the slow build-up operations at the new airport. With Malton still under-utilized in 1980 the major airlines and their customers would resist the added costs and inconvenience of the second airport and existing hotels and other service businesses would fight to hold their trade.

Further, industry would avoid the risks of locating at, or east of the new airport, as long as adjacent Metro offered attractions.

These comments may be disillusioning, but they are intended to encourage local interests to question more fully an arbitrary and premature commitment of hundreds of millions of dollars and violation of a still-emerging Toronto Centred Region Plan.

The wisdom of waiting for the "hatching" was seemingly reinforced by Donald Jamieson's announcement August 31 that there would be an independent public inquiry into the proposed airport. This would consist of an "independent board of inquiry, which would be made up of individuals outside the government service. I don't know who they would be yet" (*Globe and Mail*, September 1). However, he went on to point out that the inquiry would be made after the expropriation of the Pickering lands.

The reaction of the POP group was shown clearly in the *News Advertiser* in a headline story where the announcement was characterized "a sop for saps". The *Star* pointed out the uncomfortable closeness between the announcement and the federal election.

In a letter to the *Globe and Mail* on September 9, Stephen Roman stated:

I find it incredible that the Liberal Government actually believes the residents of Markham and Pickering Townships so gullible as to accept the recently announced Government probe of the Pickering Airport plan as anything but pure political garbage.

There is no question in my mind that the Government will do as it pleases regardless of the findings of its independent public inquiry. This is flim-flam of the worst kind. The decision has been made. Land has been acquired. The disruption has taken place. The Government, I predict, will go through with this project, but first it will put on the face of public concern, go through the charade of consultation with the people.

The key to this bamboozle is that Transport Minister Donald Jamieson says: "The inquiry will not have power to stop the airport." For that matter, I believe, neither will public opinion; only a change of government can do that. I predict the findings of this exercise will not be made known until after the next election and, from the Government's point of view, hopefully too late to affect punishment at the polls.

Scott Young pointed out that

. . . one should stop short of getting all choked up with gratitude over Transport Minister Don Jamieson giving in to public pressure and allowing an inquiry into the proposed Pickering airport. It wasn't any transcendent sense of fairness that did it, madam; it was simply the imminence of an election. That is traditionally the time for a government to map its flight-path around any flak that can be avoided. Obviously it can't send a lot of candidates out to stand there on platforms talking with a patriotic catch in the voice about participatory democracy when anybody in the crowd could identify it as a lot of bosh (if you'll pardon the abbreviation) as long as the door was being slammed on the Pickering protests.

The announcement of the election seemed to mark the end of the preliminary phases of the Pickering airport controversy. The announcement finally put a meaningful context on the statement issued by Prime Minister Trudeau in response to a POP question on Friday, March 24. The *Toronto Star* wrote:

Prime Minister Pierre Trudeau last night promised that the federal government would not go ahead with the planned Pickering airport if the majority of the people in the Toronto area don't want it.

Trudeau said: "If the majority of the people who would be served by this airport, even if only 51 per cent, didn't want this airport, then we wouldn't proceed with it."

IN CONCLUSION

The authors of this book urge the following steps:

a) The decision to establish a new Toronto area airport should be rescinded. A second airport is unnecessary at this time.

b) A prudent expansion and rearrangement of the facilities at Malton should be undertaken immediately.

c) Should there be the need for a new airport to serve the Toronto area in the future, the choice of a site should be based on proper ecological studies.

We call upon the federal government to reconsider its position and let justice and logic prevail.

APPENDIX A

A PARTIAL LIST OF CORPORATE AND PRIVATE LAND HOLDERS IN THE PICKERING AREA

MARKHAM

Regin Properties Limited, c/o Metro Trust Company, 353 Bay St. Toronto
E/S 9th line 9W 34 − 126 acres
S/S 14th Ave. 10W Parcel 1 − 10 acres
W/S Tenth Con. 9 E W Pt 3 4, E/S 10 con. 10W 4 − 77 acres
9 E 3 4 9W 34 − 102 acres
9E Pts 4 5 − 63 acres
Total acreage: 378

Markborough Properties Limited, 50 Holly St., Toronto 7
10W 14 & 15 − 187 acres
N/S 16th Ave. 9W 16 17 − 80 acres
E/S 9W ½19 − 101 acres
10W pt 20 − 91 acres
10 pt 21 − 72 acres
Total acreage: 531

Kaptyn Entreprise Limited, 3333 Bayview Ave., Suite 204, Willowdale
N/S 14th Ave. 10E pt 6 7 − 96.33 acres
Total acreage: 96.33

Dagmar Construction Limited, 2085 Midland Ave., Agincourt
E/S 10th Con 10W pt 8 − 57 acres
Total acreage: 57

Rhrian Lois Miller, Harry Miller, c/o Harry Miller, Box 464, Bmews Project, Apo, N.Y.
S/S 14th Ave. 10W 5 par 6 − 135 acres
S/S 14th Ave. 10W pt 5 Par 5 − 10 acres
Total acreage: 145

Lillian R. Dickson, P.O. Box 2131, Taipei, Taiwan, China
S/S 14th Ave. 10W Par 3 — 10 acres
Total acreage: 10

Flint-Lock Development Ltd., c/o M. Lass, 801 Eglinton Ave. W.,
Toronto
S/S 14th Ave. Con 10 E 1/4 5 — 50 acres
Total acreage: 50

Animate Construction Ltd., 2788 Bathurst St., Toronto
N/S 14th Ave. Con 9 pts 6 7 — 38 acres
Total acreage: 38

Craigman Investment Limited, c/o Rosenfeld & Schwartz,
65 Queen St., Toronto
9 con E/S 9W 7 — 10 acres
Total acreage: 10

Devondale Investment Ltd., c/o Rustic Valley Ent. Ltd.,
1400 Weston Rd., Toronto
E/S 9 con pt 8 — 50 acres

Janray Investments Ltd., c/o Rustic Valley Ent. Ltd., 1400 Weston
Rd., Toronto
W/S 10th Con 9 E pt 8 — 50 acres
W/S 10th Con 9 E   — 100 acres

Ivordale Investments Ltd., c/o Rustic Valley Ent. Ltd., 1400 Weston
Rd., Toronto
9E 10 R — 94.54 acres

Mount Olumpus Investment Ltd., c/o Rustic Valley Ent. Ltd.,
1400 Weston Rd., Toronto
acreage not known
Total acreage: 294.54

Baronspike Holdings Ltd. & Association, 85 Richmond St., Toronto
E/S 9 con pt 9 — 99.719 acres

Queenspike Holdings Ltd. & Association, c/o O'Neil, Browning, etc.,
85 Richmond St., Toronto
E/S 9th Con p 14 & 15 — 147 acres
Total acreage: 246.719

Transfer Holdings Ltd. Association, c/o Nathan Cohen, 66 Robin
Grove, Willowdale

Mark-Ten Holdings Ltd., 3101 Bathurst St., Toronto
9E 12 — 99.2 acres
Total acreage: 99.2

Newfin Land Development Ltd., 5001 Dufferin St., Toronto
9 pt 21 – 10 acres
Total acreage: 10

Chudleigh Investments Ltd., Box 100, T.D. Centre, Toronto
9E 22 – 100 acres
Total acreage: 100

Maria Gdns. Apts. Ltd., c/o George P. Longo, Barrister, 1755
Eglinton Ave., Toronto
10W 23 – 100 acres
10E 23 – 30 acres
Total acreage: 130

Granita Holdings Ltd., 5 Rubicon Ct., Willowdale
10 pt 22 – 12.66 acres
9W 26 – 10.23 acres
Total acreage: 22.89

North Brabant Investment Ltd., c/o Prousky & Prousky, 133
Richmond St., Toronto
9W 27 – 98.2 acres
Total acreage: 98.2

*Total amount of land owned by developers in Markham (in the area
involved in the Airport/Cedarwood site) is 2,366.879 acres.*

PICKERING

Century City Developments Ltd., 1 Valleybrook Dr., Don Mills
W/SDLN L23 C9 – 59 acres
C9 S½ – 42 acres
C9 L N31 – 18 acres
C9 Pt N ½ 30 – 77 acres
C9 N½ – 100 acres
C9 23 – 36 acres
C9 L24 – 52 acres
Total acreage: 384

Guieseppe Lombardo, 55 Churchill Ave., Toronto 3
C9 pt S½ L25 par 1 – 15.24 acres
Total acreage: 15.24

Karl Franz Czanka, c/o Miss Herta Steinmueller, 100 High Park Ave.,
Toronto
C9 Pt S½ L25 Pt. 3 – 9.13 acres
Total acreage: 9.13

Una Monaghan, c/o J.W.L. Monaghan Personnel, 1480 Don Mills Rd., Don Mills
C9 pt S½ L25 pt. 4 − 13.0 acres
Total acreage: 13.0

Blue Orchard Holdings Ltd., 3311 Bayview Ave., Suite 102, Willowdale
C8 N½ 26 & NE ¼ RA between 26 & 27 − 100 acres
C8 N½ L26 − 2 acres
C8 26 & 27 − 48 acres
Total acreage: 150

Warchester Investments Ltd., Dortan Holdings Ltd., c/o Prousky & Prousky, 133 Richmond St. W., Toronto
C 8 S 3¼ 21 W/SDN 21 − 147.51 acres
Bropa Holdings Ltd., Warchester Investments Ltd., Prousky & Prousky, etc.
C4 pt N½ L30 − 75 acres
Total acreage: 222.51

Pickonto Holdings Ltd., 3311 Bayview Ave., Toronto
C7 Pt N½ 26 E/S sideline 27 − 100 acres
Total acreage: 100

Mogol Bldg. Entr. Ltd., 225156 Properties Ltd., 244 Finch Ave. W., Willowdale
C8 S½ 22 N/8th − 133.05 acres
Total acreage: 133.05

Mash Investment Ltd., c/o 53 Prince Arthur St., Toronto 5
C8 pt L23 − 1 acre − Par. 1

Toe-Jam Holdings Ltd., c/o 53 Prince Arthur St., Toronto
C8 pt L23 − 1 acre − Par. 2

Karjenjo Investment Ltd., c/o 53 Prince Arthur St., Toronto
C8 pt L23 − 1 acre − Par. 3

Iona Silverberg, c/o 53 Prince Arthur St., Toronto
C8 pt L23 Parcel 75 − 1 acre

Marilyn Merrick, c/o 53 Prince Arthur St., Toronto
C8 Pt L23 Parcel 74 − 1 acre

Susan Young, c/o 53 Prince Arthur St., Toronto
C8 Pt L23 Parcel 73 − 1 acre
Parcels 72 − 38 of L23 Con 8

Paul Merrick, c/o 53 Prince Arthur St., Toronto
C8 Pt L23 Parcel 76 − 6 acres
Parcels 77 − 116 one acre

Loring Development Ltd., 5001 Dufferin St., Downsview
C8 s½ 24 E/SDLN — 15 acres
Total acreage: 15

Birnardi Holding Corp. Ltd.,
Jenmill Invest. Ltd.,
Carrity Invest. Ltd.,
Bea-Mel Assets Ltd.,
Uranus Invest. Ltd., c/o Singer Keyfetz Cass etc., P.O. Box 256,
Royal Trust Tower, T.D. Centre, Toronto
C 3 N/S C3 S½ L27 — 104.75 acres
C 3 N/S — 4 acres
Total acreage: 108.75

Cembre Investments Ltd., Jenmill Investments Ltd., Carrity
Investments Ltd., 121 Richmond St. W., Ste. 804, Toronto
C4 S½ L25 — 100 acres
C4 S½ L25 — 10 acres
Total acreage: 110

Aztecana Corporation Ltd., 31 Fallingbrook Cres., Toronto
C4 Pt S½ L22 — 97 acres

Hallmark Investments Ltd., 1884 Eglinton Ave. E., Scarborough
C5 Pt S½ L26 — 87.84 acres
Total acreage: 87.84

Leslie Estates Thornhill Ltd., c/o David Mclean Ltd., 74 Steeles Ave.,
Thornhill
C5 S½ L21 — 97.43 acres
C5 S½ L21 — 2 acres
(June 1972, changed to Resort Hotels Ltd., R.R. 2, Gormley.)
Total acreage: 99.43

Circumference Investment Ltd.,
c/o Murray White, 5 Highmount Dr.,
Willowdale
C5 S½ of S½ L25 — 50 acres
Total acreage: 50

Harry Fisher Holdings, Rickie Realty Ltd., 995 Eglinton Ave.,
Toronto
C5 Pt L33 — 10 acres, 72.72 acres, 18.76 acres
Total acreage: 101.48

Crifo Antonio, De Luca Francesco,
c/o Trinacria Travel Agency,
1769 Danforth Ave., Toronto
C6 Pt L29 — 25 acres
Total acreage: 25

Domingo Holdings Ltd., G & B Scarborough Holdings, c/o Berman
& Rosenblatt, 121 Richmond St., Toronto
C6 Pt L 24 – 60.55 acres
Total acreage: 60.55

Vicross Apartments Ltd.,
Helene Francis Investments Ltd.,
Elderwood Realties Ltd.,
Krehem, Herman,
Rutman, Samuel, c/o S.A. Glick, 2788 Bathurst St., Toronto
C6 Pt L31 – 159.45 acres
                    15.00 acres

Villarboit Holdings Ltd., c/o Dr. G. Goyd, 2811 Keele St.,
Downsview
C6 Pt L25 – 102.50 acres
C6 Pt L26 – 100 acres
Total acreage: 202.50

Picklare Development Ltd., c/o Kelner Cooper & Sitt, 120 Adelaide
St., Toronto
C7 Pt L25 – 90.0 acres

Captain Development Ltd., 3333 Bayview Ave., Toronto
C6 Pt L 34 S 7th – 10.2 acres
C6 Pt L 33 – 13.0 acres
C6 Pt L33 – 10.850 acres
C6 Pt L 33 – 10.6 acres
C6 Pt L 33 – 10.3 acres

John Kaptyn, 3333 Bayview Ave., Toronto
C6 Pt L 34 – 77.6 acres
              –   8.98 acres
C6 Pt L 35 – 21.2 acres
C6 Pt L 33 – 59.45 acres

Maddox, Grace E., 3333 Bayview Ave., Toronto
C6 Pt L 33 – 10.2 acres
C6 Pt L33 – 10.17 acres
C6 Pt L33 – 10.8 acres
C6 Pt L33 – 11.5 acres

Runnymede Development Corporation, 45 Parliament St., Toronto
C3 Pt L24 & Pt RA – 175.89 acres
C3 Pt L24 Pt RA
C3 Pt S½ LTS 24 & 25 Pt RA – 10 acres
Total acreage: 185.89

Portstaff Properties Ltd., Barry Michael Chapman, 104 Bidewell St., Downsview
SDLN 31 W/S C3 Pt S½ L31 − 76.160 acres

Longstaff Investment Ltd., 104 Bidewell (changed to 21 Vintage Lane, Toronto, June 1972)
Altona Road, C3 pt L32 − 98.82 acres. E/S

Coconut Investment Ltd., 104 Bidewell St., Downsview
Altona Road W/S − 8.731 acres
Altona Road W/S C 3 Pt L 33 − 96.833

Tomahawk Investment Ltd., 104 Bidewell St., Downsview
C3 N/S Cen Pt L 34 − 130.00 acres
C3 N/S − 5 acres

Tona Investments Ltd., c/o Barry Chapman, 104 Bidewell St., Downsview, (c/o Gordon Carton, 1810 Avenue Rd., Toronto 12)
C4 S½ Lt 34 − 11.399 acres
C4 S½ L34 − 10 acres

UXBRIDGE

Century City Development Ltd., 1 Valleybrook Dr., Don Mills
2,137 acres

Casa Malona Ltd., c/o Wm. Morris, R.R. 3, Stouffville
C1 W½ of L8 − 92 acres
　　　　　　− 20 acres
Total acreage: 112

Total amount of land owned by developers in Uxbridge is 2,249 acres.

APPENDIX B

SUBMISSION TO THE GOVERNMENTS OF CANADA AND ONTARIO CONCERNING THE PROPOSED AIRPORT II AND THE NORTH PICKERING COMMUNITY

THE CENTRAL ONTARIO CHAPTER OF THE TOWN PLANNING INSTITUTE OF CANADA

JULY, 1972

A. Introduction

The Central Ontario Chapter of the Town Planning Institute of Canada is an organization representing approximately three hundred professional planners who practise within the Toronto region. The members of the Institute have a professional interest in decisions relating to planning affecting the area in which they work. The decisions by the Governments of Canada and Ontario to locate a second international airport to the east of Metropolitan Toronto and to establish a new urban community adjacent to this airport are clearly of major importance to the future form of urban settlement of the Toronto Centred Region.

The Chapter is interested in the process by which decisions are made because we believe that decisions are shaped by the process used in making them. In previous submissions, we have supported a process which involves four fundamental steps common to any planning situation. These include:

1. Background studies designed to determine the need for change;
2. The development of alternative forms of meeting specific needs and the comparison of the socio-economic and environmental implications of each;
3. Public review of the alternatives to assure a full understanding by the public of the implications and to assure that all relevant problems are dealt with;
4. The refinement and reiteration of steps one, two and three until a final choice can be made.

Our review is based on scarce public information which has been difficult to obtain and in some cases available only for very cursory perusal. (We understand that an offer was made by the Ministry of Transport to give the Town Planning Institute of Canada a full technical briefing. Unfortunately, this offer was not communicated to the executive of the Central Ontario Chapter before this brief was substantially complete. While we would be interested in learning as much as possible about the technical background, we believe that the comments made here are more concerned with process and public communication than with purely technical matters.) Notwithstanding the paucity of information we wish to make the following comments on the process.

B. Background Studies

Need studies have established that significant new capacity must be provided to accommodate future air passenger traffic in the Toronto region. The case for providing this capacity at a second airport rather than through the expansion of Malton is, however, less conclusive. In view of the concerns expressed later in this submission, it is particularly significant that the need for a second international airport rather than large scale expansion of Malton is based directly on the principle that *because of the nuisance they generate, major airport facilities should not be situated close to existing or future urbanized areas.*

C. The Alternatives

In order to solve the capacity problem, the Federal Government in 1968 undertook extensive reviews of alternate sites, after a previous decision to expand Malton was reversed. Following a preliminary review of some fifty-nine sites, expansion at Malton and four other sites were extensively reviewed. Cost benefit studies indicated that expansion at Malton would be substantially cheaper by perhaps one and a half billion dollars. The site ultimately chosen in North Pickering was not evaluated at this stage.

The Provincial Government apparently rejected all five sites partly because of the nuisance problem that would be generated at Malton and partly because it sought to use the development potential of a new airport to implement the development plan for the Toronto Centred Region which proposed a shift of urban settlement to the east of Metropolitan Toronto, to Oshawa, Port Hope and Cobourg. It is at this point that several weaknesses emerge in the analysis of alternatives:

1. The decision that a second airport is needed appears to have been taken without adequate consideration of the potential of Malton in the broad context of possible improvements in ground access, future changes in aircraft technology, and the possibility of shifting large volumes of regional passenger traffic to high-speed surface transportation systems.

We are also concerned about apparent contradictions in the following two government statements about the need for a second airport:

"It was demonstrated that some 35,000 people were already affected by noise from flight operations and that the proposed expansion of Malton would subject an *additional* 35,000 people in existing residential communities to this noise." (Press Release — W.D. McKeough, June 6, 1971.)

"No additions to the present noise lands are expected if the expansion of the present facility is undertaken. Thus there will be no additional infringement on the environmental quality of the area." (Toronto Airport Location: Proposed Malton Expansion (Confidential), September 15, 1970.)

2. The North Pickering Site *was not evaluated* in the same terms as the preferred five alternatives, but only against a new southwestern alternative located in Beverley Township west of Hamilton. The evaluation which has been made public is mainly concerned with the relative effect of the two sites on implementing the Toronto Centred Region concept, and is based only on a cursory transportation analysis and an even more cursory study of the ecological features.

3. From the material which has been made available it appears that the proposed airport at North Pickering is likely, if anything, to stimulate development adjacent to and relating to Metropolitan Toronto rather than in the areas further east. *There is some doubt as to the efficacy of the airport in promoting the development concept of the Toronto-Centred Region.* (For example, given the location of the two airports and the necessity of providing highly efficient transportation links between them, it is possible that the most desirable location for many firms could be Richmond Hill. Development in this location could be a serious threat to the Toronto Centred Region plan.)

4. We believe that both the Provincial and Federal Governments must uphold the principle that *major airport facilities are incompatible with nearby urban settlements* and that it is preferable to avoid possible disturbances to people and activities by locating any major airport in areas which will remain unsettled in the future through the provision of special purpose ground transportation for major concentrations of people in the Region. In this regard, we believe that a comparison of the future noise implications of both the expansion of Malton and the Malton/Pickering combination should be undertaken — or made public if such a comparison has already been done.

5. We consider that inadequate measures have been taken to avoid a repetition of the noise problem in urban areas around Malton. We note the statement which has recently been released by the Province, that "Site F" (North Pickering) *contains the seeds of heavy noise impacts on future urban areas in the manner of Malton.*" We also note that this statement has not been further alluded to in any other public presentation, and that no evidence has been presented as to the degree of noise which may be expected in the affected communities.

Notwithstanding this admitted danger, little has been done to avert it. The Federal Government will purchase only the approximately eighteen thousand acres of land required for the airport site and will not protect the critical noise lands beyond the site through land acquisition as they have done in Ste. Scholastique. The responsibility of restricting the use of these lands has been left to the Provincial Government which has used its power under the Planning Act of land use control by Ministerial order. We do not consider that this method of protecting vulnerable lands represents a guarantee that a subsequent Minister or Government may not modify or rescind the existing protective orders. We are particularly concerned about the use of this technique in light of the opinion of the Ontario Law Reform Commission that ". . .the Planning Act does not confer power on the Government of Ontario to institute changes in Official Plans on its own initiative." (Ontario Law Reform Commission "Report on Development Control," 1971.)

While we recognize that a future government might also decide to sell lands it owns outright, we think this point reinforces our view that the most powerful planning tools must be employed to ensure that vulnerable lands are protected from undesirable development such as is currently permitted in Mississauga and Etobicoke.

6. We believe that the use of land for a "Parkway Belt" and for industrial activities is insufficient as a buffer between residential areas and the airport facilities. Furthermore, the people who will work or who will use parkland adjacent to the airport should also receive adequate protection from aircraft noise.

We also question the validity of the Provincial Government acquiring approximately ten thousand acres of land at an estimated cost of thirty million dollars to be used as a "Parkway Belt" or service corridor between the Airport – North Pickering complex and Metropolitan Toronto. It is possible that a significant portion of the ten thousand acres will have to be used for expressway, rapid transit facilities and hydro rights-of-way leaving an insignificant portion to fulfill the increasing needs of the recreation and leisure activities of the people living in the Toronto Region. We are concerned that the Provincial Government's interest in providing airport-related facilities within the Parkway Belt could inhibit the socially more beneficial use of this land for Regional Park purposes.

7. We question the advisability of committing large amounts of money to implement the Government's development concept without reference to a formally constituted Provincial Plan for the Toronto Centred Region. We believe that a provincially prepared plan determining the settlement pattern in the Toronto Region and directly affecting the well being and capital expenditures of local and regional municipalities must be made "official" before being implemented.

D. The Public Debate
We must stress the importance of public debate in the planning

process. We not only believe that it removes suspicion and makes implementation easier, but we also firmly believe that it contributes substantively to the understanding of the issues at hand. We are therefore very concerned with the refusal of the Federal Minister of Transport to consider the possibility that a second airport might not be required or that a better site might be found. We also believe that it is wrong in principle and unsatisfactory in practice for the Provincial Government to make unilateral decisions without prior consultation with and commitments from the affected local municipalities. Although both governments have attempted to inform professional and technical groups of the reasons behind their decisions, we do not believe that this is a substitute for providing the public at large with a formal opportunity to contribute to the debate.

E. Submission

On the basis of the argument presented above, we respectfully request that:

1. The Government of Canada re-examine and publicly present its findings on the need for a second new airport in the Toronto region with particular concern for preventing any disturbing impact on existing and future urbanized areas.

2. In order to facilitate a public appraisal the Government of Ontario suspend all agreements with the Government of Canada concerning the second international airport.

3. The Government of Ontario initiate a public appraisal through the use of public meetings of the impact of major airports on urbanized and non-urbanized areas within the Province.

4. Before making a final decision on the location of a new community such as North Pickering, the Provincial Government complete a formally constituted plan for the Toronto Centred Region.

5. The Government of Ontario develop a mechanism for the public scrutiny of Provincial Plans in a manner similar to the requirements under the Planning Act which are applicable to all municipalities.

We recognize that without the airport at the proposed location, the Province would lose the implied subsidy for water, sewer, and ground transportation services from the Federal Government and therefore would assume a greater initial cost in establishing the North Pickering Community. We are also aware of the delays created by increased public participation and the apparent, but not insuperable risks of increased costs through land speculation. Yet from the information available, we conclude that the Federal Government is trying to satisfy its need for additional airport capacity by helping the Provincial Government satisfy its desire to establish a new urban community east of Metropolitan Toronto.

106

The Provincial Government in turn appears to justify the investment in land and services for the North Pickering Community by assuming that the airport will act as a catalyst for growth and development in this area, although it has not yet been proved conclusively that the airport would serve in this way. We believe that the logic of this compromise is faulty, may not be in the public interest, and that a review is essential.

SOURCE NOTES

Chapter 2 The Need

1 Regional Development Branch, Department of Treasury and Economics, Ontario, "Regional Impact of a New International Airport for Toronto", March 1970, p. 81.

2 *Ibid*, pp. 81-2.

3 *Ibid.*, p. 81.

4 S.G. Larliere and F.E. Tarema, "Impact of Projected Air Travel Demand on Airport Access", *Highway Research Record*, Washington National Research Council, 1969, No. 274, p. 24.

5 *Limits to Growth* (Boston: Massachusetts Institute of Technology, 1972).

6 Capt. J. Desmarais, "The Case Against Pickering", *Canadian Aviation*, June 1970, pp. 20-2.

7 Toronto Airport Planning Team, Canadian Air Transportation Administration, Ministry of Transport, "Technical Report", September 1970, p. 39.

8 "Jamaica Bay and Kennedy Airport—A Multi-Disciplinary Environmental Study", p. 120. The year being used as a basis of comparison was 1967. Total movements have increased 14 per cent from 1967-70.

9 *Ibid.*

10 Toronto Airport Planning Team, *op. cit.*, p. 39.

11 G. Hall, Travel Editor, *The Toronto Star*, March 1, 1972, p. 6.

Chapter 3 The Choice

1 Federal Department of Transport, Hon. Paul Hellyer, "Toronto International Airport, Toronto 1930-1968".

2 Department of Transport, "A Study Outline to Determine the Location of the Site for a Second Airport to Serve Metropolitan Toronto", May 1969.

3 Province of Ontario, "Regional Impact of a New International Airport for Toronto", March 1970, p.1.

4 P. Beinhacker, "Advisory Review, Toronto International Airport", May 11, 1970.

5 "Strategy Paper Relating Aviation Systems to Broad Policies and Programmes of Public and Private Sectors", September 8, 1970.

Province of Ontario, "Summary Report on Status of Airport Planning (Toronto II)", May 1970.

Ibid., p. 19.

"Strategy Paper Relating Aviation Systems to Broad Policies and Programmes of Public and Private Sectors", September 8, 1970.

"Toronto Airport II Site Evaluation Report, Pickering Township Site", pp. 5, 6, 9.

0 "Definition of Site Envelops Southwest and Northeast Airport Sites", August 20, 1971, pp. 2, 6.

1 Letter from A.A. Speer to G.E. McDowell, August 11, 1971.

2 Province of Ontario, "Review of Proposed Airport Sites E and F, Regional Development Plan", October 1971, p. 3.

Note: There is a large series of reports, letters, etc., released by the government, which groups activities in 1970. Some of the chronology of the reports is upset because of the inclusion of work done previously but reported at a later date.